We Are Never Alone

We Are Never Alone:

Reassuring Insights from the Other Side

Anthony Quinata

4th Dimension Press ■ Virginia Beach ■ Virginia

Dedicated to my mother, Rosalia, and my father, Antonio—soul mates on the Other Side. I miss you.

To my sisters, Meridith and Nadine, and my brothers, Edward and Steve, and their families.

My love for all of you will never die.

And for you who are grieving.

Worn

I'm tired; I'm worn.
My heart is heavy
From the work it takes
To keep on breathing.
I've made mistakes.
I let my hope fail.
My soul feels crushed
By the weight of this world.

And I know that you can give me rest
So I cry out with all that I have left.

Let me see redemption win.
Let me know the struggle ends
That you can mend a heart
That's frail and torn.
I wanna know that a song can rise
From the ashes of a broken life
And [that what's dead] can be reborn
'Cause I'm worn.

Lyrics by Tenth Av

Contents

Acknowledgments

While I was writing this book, I told God and the souls that once I was finished, I was ready to go home. The peals of laughter I heard told me that God and the souls have a sense of humor, even though I was serious.

As I look back, I realize that if it wasn't for them, the prayers of Mary, mother of Jesus, my family and friends, here and on the Other Side, I'm not sure how I would have made it through this chapter of my life. Thank you.

Thank you, Camille and Steve Massing, for all of your love and support along the way.

Thank you, Donna Nikolla and Marianne Shotto, for your friendship and for listening.

To my "Facebook friends" who have become real friends, to those who trusted me enough to reconnect with their loved ones on the Other Side, to those who trusted me enough to ask questions about the Other Side, and to the souls who gave me the answers—thank you.

I love you.

Preface

I don't normally work at psychic fairs, but I was at Cornerstone Books for the store's Halloween metaphysical fair. The store had changed hands by that time. Deb Guinther, whom I talked about in my book *Communications from the Other Side*, wasn't the owner any longer. It was now owned by Jenny Vega and her husband, Angel.

There was a lull in the number of people wanting readings so the other readers and I were sitting around talking. "I wish Rick was here," Cathy, one of the card readers, said.

"Why?" Samantha, another reader asked her.

"I was hoping he would read my palm for me," Cathy replied.

"I can read your palm," Jenny said, which surprised us all.

"Can you really?" Cathy asked. Jenny nodded so Cathy held up her right hand and asked, "Will I live a long life?"

Jenny looked at her palm and nodded, "Oh yes, you'll live a long life."

Samantha, who was sitting next to me, held up her hand and asked

"What about me? Will I live a long life?"

Jenny gazed at her hand before she said, smiling, "Oh yes, you'll live a very long, healthy life."

It was the word "healthy" that prompted me to hold up my hand. "What about me, Jenny? I just had a physical, and when I left, the doctor gave me a calendar, but it goes only to May of next year. What's he trying to tell me?"

Everyone laughed as Jenny looked closely at my hand. "Angel, come here and look at his hand!"

Angel walked over, looked at my hand, and his eyes grew large. "Man, you died, crossed over, and came back. Did you know that?" he asked excitedly.

"I've always had a feeling," I told him. When I was five years old, I had to have surgery. I have no idea now what it was for, but I do remember not liking the mask on my face as the doctor was telling me a story. I tried to push the mask away because I was feeling sleepy.

Several years later my mother told the story of how the surgeon walked up to her and asked if she believed in God. "Yes, I do," she told him.

"Then I suggest that you go to the chapel and pray," he said as gently as he could. "I don't know if your son is going to make it or not."

My mother never did say, and I can't be sure, but I believe it had something to do with an asthma attack. I was asthmatic from the time I was about three months old.

My mother went to the chapel and prayed like she had never prayed before, and kept praying until the surgeon found her there. She was relieved to see that he was smiling this time. He told her I would pull through after all.

At that time we lived in Wilmington, California in a housing project that's no longer there. When you walked through the front door, the kitchen was to the left, and the living room was on the right with a stairway in the middle leading to the second floor. I can still remember sitting on those stairs giving a lot of thought to my birthday coming up the next day. It was not only going to be my sixth birthday, but my brother Eddie's first birthday, as well, since we both shared the same birth day.

I came to a decision, sitting there on those stairs. I had an announcement to make, and I knew it wasn't going to go over well. "Mom, go ahead and celebrate Eddie's birthday tomorrow, but you don't have to celebrate mine anymore," I announced to her after much thought.

"Don't be silly," she told me. "You're going to have a birthday party too." She sounded agitated. I knew that my mother wouldn't agree to what I was suggesting, but I really didn't care about celebrating my birthday. I will admit being grateful the next day that we did though.

I found out years later that loss of interest in birthdays is common with people who have been through what is referred to as a "near-death experience." Angel seemed to confirm for me what I had believed for years.

"You crossed over and came back with knowledge you're meant to share with the rest of us," Angel continued, looking closely at my palm.

I wondered what he meant by "us." I couldn't help but smile when I thought this.

Angel must have known what I was thinking because he looked at me seriously and said, "With the world, man. You're supposed to share what you know with the world."

Seven months later in May, I was sitting in front of Rick with my hand outstretched, palm up. My book was scheduled to be released later that year, and I was hoping to get an idea as to how it would go. "I don't see you doing the medium thing for long," Lawrence told me.

"Really? What do you see me doing?" I asked him.

"Teaching . . . I see you teaching."

"And what exactly am I supposed to be teaching?" I asked. I had planned to do the "medium thing" for at least five years after my book came out.

"I don't know," he said. I can only tell you what I'm seeing here in your 'Mound of Mercury.'" After he said that, I could tell by the look on his face that the reading was over.

I got up and walked away, thinking about what Angel had said to me seven months before. "You crossed over and came back with knowledge you're meant to share with the rest of us—not just us, but with the world, man."

Making the transition that Rick predicted wasn't easy for me. Getting me to do so was an uphill battle for the souls. They got my attention the only way they could . . . by slowly causing the requests for readings with me to gradually come to a grinding halt.

Prologue
by Sofia Pico-Ambrosio

Just prior to meeting my husband Anthony, I had recently given up on a twelve-year marriage. It had not been a very fulfilling or supportive marriage, to say the least. In fact, I was at the lowest point in my life. I felt as if I were dead inside. There was no joy, no hope, and no self-esteem. I had no idea that my life was about to change drastically.

The minute I met Anthony, I was convinced that I knew him but could not think of how. I reviewed my whole life and could not explain it. I just knew that I knew him. Months later he let me in on a secret. He had seen in his meditations that I was going to be coming into his life. He knew where and about when we would meet and that I was of Spanish descent with short, curly brown hair.

He was an amazing person who was incredibly funny, kind, generous, caring, nonjudgmental, supportive, incredibly intelligent, and an "open book" as he would say, a true friend, (I could go on and on . . .).

On top of all of this, he was also an amazing and talented healer. Gods' healing energy streamed through his hands. *Of course*, God used him to channel His energy. Anthony's heart and intent were as pure as no other I've ever seen! He was a chiropractor who decided he was going to create a practice, different from any other, where the goal was to get people well enough that they wouldn't need to come back. This demanded a huge sacrifice on his part which required much longer hours and produced a much lower income than the average chiropractor. Needless to say, it worked. People, who had used many other therapies and had not found success in relieving their pain, diseases, or other conditions, finally found it with him. Without spending a penny in advertising, he had a full practice with a year–long waiting list, all from word–of–mouth referrals. I can't tell you how many times I have met people who had nothing but adoring things to tell me about Anthony once they knew I was his wife. They would say, "He changed my life. He helped me with an emotional problem I'd had all my life. Oh, and he also fixed my back!!!!!!" He would spend countless unpaid hours just talking to people, giving them hope and spiritual advice. Even the cable guy, who came to hook up Anthony's service, was so appreciative of his help that he gave him his personal number and said, "If you ever need any help with anything, call me anytime."

People were extremely grateful because they had never experienced someone going out of his way to help them as Anthony had done. He didn't care about money. He cared about people! Of the patients he had treated who had cancer and tumors, eleven experienced a near or full reversal of the disease. And he always made people laugh. This was part of the package. He also successfully treated numerous so-called "incurable" conditions and diseases with just his "bare hands." And he never took credit for it. He always said, "The Big Guy (pointing to the sky) did it."

Being around Anthony was like a ray of sunshine. I could not wait until I got to see him again.

Eventually we started dating, and my life took a complete 180 degree turn. I went from feeling unloved to experiencing the deepest, most fulfilling, supportive, and passionate pure love I have ever known. It was everything I had ever hoped for and more! Our lives were filled with affection, meaningful conversation, and laughter so unbridled that it made me cry and caused spasms of the abdominal muscles. He worked very hard to repair my broken self. Every day he told me that I was beautiful and how much he loved me. Many times he said, "I don't want a day to go by without telling you that 'I Love You!'" My life was complete.

Then he started getting sick more and more often. He thought it was food poisoning from restaurant food, but I had a bad feeling. Despite my urging him, he didn't want to go to a medical doctor. Maybe he knew it was going to be bad news. Actually, he told me how, when he was a little boy, he would tell his mother, "I'm going to die young, so you better get used to it." He was also gifted with a keen sense of intuition.

We married in July of 2004, and the following January he was in the hospital fighting for his life. He was hooked up to every monitor and medical machine you could imagine. He was in an induced coma due to a severe bout of pancreatitis, among other things. Unbelievably, he recovered and was released from the hospital eleven days later. The doctors and nurses were amazed as even his kidneys had stopped working at one point.

As the years went by, we visited doctors of every kind—sometimes getting results, sometimes not. He had been misdiagnosed as having diabetes and was experiencing recurring bouts of pancreatitis. The pain you feel with pancreatitis has been described to us as natural childbirth or amputation without anesthesia.

He fought as hard as he could to try to stay alive. Despite working twelve hour days on a regular basis, he would exercise on the treadmill before work and go to the health club to sit in the sauna after work. He changed his diet, took loads of supplements, and even took medications he didn't agree with. He didn't want to "die on me." He lived for years with his triglycerides over 2,000. Sometimes they went over 3,000. According to the AMA, healthy triglyceride levels are supposed to be 150 or under. Anything over that can cause heart disease and strokes. He was clearly a walking time bomb. In addition, he had very high levels of iron in his blood. We saw medical doctors, specialists, toxicologists, acupuncturists, and a medical intuitive. Since I was a massage therapist and an energy worker, I gave him treatments whenever he would allow me to. Some things helped for a while and then stopped working. Other treatments actually made him ill. We exhausted our funds since we had a high deductible insurance, and most of his expenses were out of pocket.

Our dear friends Sherry and Gordon Shayne convinced us to go to their amazing naturopathic doctor in Colorado Springs named Mark Cooper. Since we were very low on funds, Sherry and Gordon generously offered to cover the costs for Anthony's initial treatments with Mark. Finally Mark Cooper, after spending countless hours researching his case, found out what he had. We were very excited to hear the news and that we would finally know what was making him sick. Mark said, "Well, there's good news and there's bad news. The good news is that I know what you have. The bad news is that it is a rare genetic disease that has no known treatment or cure." That was a heavy blow to take. Mark let us know that there were things we could try, but of course, there were no guarantees. Mark explained how he thought things would progress for Anthony. Eventually, the high triglycerides in his blood would prevent enough oxygen from nourishing his vital organs, and he would basically asphyxiate. He was the only doctor who was able to explain this to us and did it with compassion and concern.

As time went by, we tried to live our lives to the fullest. It was as if Anthony knew his time on earth would be very limited. He studied every possible theory, ideology, religion, and healing method. Anything relating to God, he knew or would learn. He lived in the moment which was wonderful but at times was upsetting to me, especially if he missed or was late for an anniversary or birthday dinner. His response was, "I lost track of time." He often ran behind during his appointments, but most people didn't mind since they knew that when it got to be their turn, he would give them 100 per cent of his attention. He didn't let people walk out the door if he wasn't satisfied with how their bodies had responded to the treatment.

Although very sick and getting weaker after each bout of pancreatitis, he continued to work extremely long hours, as he knew his patients needed him. I was in a state of denial (a coping mechanism) thinking that for sure God would not let him die, considering all of the people he was helping and saving (including me). I believed God would continue to save him and eventually heal him. The time came when with greater frequency he suffered from more bouts of pancreatitis, often screaming at the top of his lungs in pain—sometimes ending up at the hospital, sometimes not. Many times we both thought this was the one that would take him out. However, he kept surviving them against all odds, until the last time. He died in my arms on August 14, 2011. It was exactly one month before his forty-second birthday.

As he had been an extraordinary person in life, he turned out to be also extraordinary after death. Because he died at home, paramedics and the police came to the house and then the coroner took his body away. I cannot put into words the way I felt at that time. Frantic, I decided to start vacuuming as I figured many people would be coming to the house. Then I heard Anthony's voice say, "Calm down. Lie down. I want to show you something." Not knowing what to think, but trusting what I heard, I laid down on the couch. Then I felt (his) energy merge into mine. Every cell, molecule, of my being was vibrating. With that, he was telling me, "I will never leave you!" Then I was able to get a glimpse of where he was. I felt an incredible feeling of joy and elation—more than I had ever experienced. Then I felt the freedom he felt in being out of his "miserable body" (as he would often refer to it). The incredible pain and suffering he had felt during his life had been lifted! He helped many by relieving pain that they thought they would never be free of. He did this while no one was able to relieve his pain . . . until now!

For about a year and a half, he continued to talk to me. I could hear him as clearly as if he were standing right next to me (he was, and is!). The beauty of this was that now he was able to be with me 24/7! There was no more waiting late at night for him to get home only to find that he was exhausted and just wanting to collapse on the couch. Now he was with me no matter where I went! Of course I was still devastated by his loss and went through (and still going through) deep grief. Even though I was overwrought with sadness and despair, I remember thinking of other widows and how difficult it must be to not hear and experience their loved one as I was able to. I couldn't imagine suddenly experiencing a loss such as that without receiving any signs "from beyond." I have many magical moments where he came through for me "from the Other Side." For example, last February I went to

Chicago to learn the Bengston Energy Healing Method. Actually it was during a session with a medium that Anthony told me to learn this technique. Anyway, it was Valentine's Day. It was very cute and touching to see that everywhere I went, there were many men frantically running around to buy flowers, chocolates, and cards for their wives/girlfriends. Then I was a little sad to think that I wouldn't be getting any of those things. I thought to myself, "I guess I won't be getting any flowers from my baby this year." Since I had some time to kill before the workshop, I decided to walk around the vicinity of the hotel to see what there was in the area. It was downtown Chicago amidst the hustle and bustle of a big city and during a busy time of day. Still a bit sad, I had my head down. I took a few steps and there, right in my path, was a perfect beautiful yellow carnation! All of the sudden it was as if the time stopped and the busyness of the city faded away. That took my breath away! I knew it was from Anthony and I could feel him smiling! Yes, I still have it!

I continued to experience remarkable things and hear Anthony talking to me but eventually the frequency and intensity diminished. Anthony told me that it was for my own good. Now that I was getting stronger, he was able to pull away a bit so I could continue to heal. If he didn't, I would become too dependent on that type of contact and would not progress. I understood. After three years, I still "know" that he is watching me at times but do not always feel him.

Over the course of these last three years, I have had readings with various mediums. They are all different in the way they receive information. Some are good at receiving certain information; others are good at relaying other messages. They all have had valuable messages that have helped me grow from where I was at that time.

I was sharing some of my experiences with my friend Cathy who had known Anthony. She told me about an amazing psychic medium she knew in Denver named Anthony Quinata (to avoid confusion, I will refer to him as Anthony Q). Instantly I knew I had to go see him. Not only did I like his first name, but I had a really strong feeling that he was going to help me greatly.

As my husband's birthday was approaching and since I hadn't heard him "talk to me" in quite some time, I thought it would be a good way to celebrate his special day by scheduling a reading with Anthony

Quinata. Anthony Q did not know anything about me other than my name.

The session began, and right away my father–in–law, Domenico, showed up. His son's death (my husband) had been very hard on him. He was eighty–six but didn't look it. He was still working as an anesthesiologist and several times a week would go to the gym to spend several hours there working out and doing yoga, Pilates, or whatever class they offered. However he did have some health issues including COPD, had a pacemaker, and had had his prostate removed due to cancer. But these things didn't slow him down. It was the emotional burden of having to bury his only son that, I believe, eventually led to his death just about a year after Anthony died. Since my own father had passed away thirteen years prior, I saw Domenico as my dad and was extremely happy to hear from him. Anthony Q said, "You were close to your father–in–law? Because he's the one stepping forward . . . " And then he said, "Where's the Marie . . . " I broke into tears. Marie is my mother–in–law. My heart aches for her as she not only buried her one–and–only loving son whom she adored, but a year later lost her own husband! Then he said to, "Please tell Marie, because he's calling out to Marie, that you've heard from your father–in–law!!!"

Anthony Q kept getting accurate details about Domenico, describing his personality to a "T" and said several times throughout the session that he kept referring to himself as my father! That made me smile! Anthony Q also asked if Domenico had heart and lung issues. To both questions which I said, "Yes." Then Anthony Q said, "COPD"! Right again!

Then Anthony Q said, "You lost a husband?" I broke out in tears again. "His son?" he asked. "Yes! " Apparently they had decided that Domenico should talk first to give me the message about Marie, and also because once my Anthony began to speak, he wouldn't be able to get a word in! That is how Anthony was in life. He always had a lot to say! He talked about a birthday, and I confirmed that my husband's birthday would be the following day. "Then the timing is perfect," he said. Anthony Q told me that my Anthony was playing music for him (my Anthony loved music and played the guitar). Then he said that Anthony called himself a real romantic and that ours was his first marriage and the second for me. All correct! "He keeps wanting me to tell you how much he loves you"! Anthony Q said. Anthony Q tried to get his name and then laughed and said my Anthony told him "Anthony, like you! He said he likes me because we have the same name! He's funny! He has a great sense of humor. He's a real jokester. He liked to kid around because he's kidding now! He's having a lot of fun!" Clearly he was connected with my husband and his father and was hearing their messages very accurately.

Anthony Q went on to talk about many other things that were accurate. Occasionally stating, "Boy, he loves you! He just loves you so . . . so . . . much; he doesn't want you to forget that! You were his first one and only." He talked about the new car I recently got. The previous car I had while Anthony was still alive was a nice car. I bought it used, but it constantly had one problem after another. I was so nervous about this that when getting this new one, I asked Anthony to help me pick out one that would be reliable. In fact, while driving the new car home, I felt an energy lifting off of me and the new car. I then realized that he and maybe others had been working to make sure that the old car would not break down on me again. That energy was no longer needed!!!! What a relief! And what a blessing! Anthony Q said, "He is very happy that you have this new car and that you are taking care of yourself. He said that the other car was a clunker! He said he helped you pick it out because you asked him too! And it's blue?" Yes, yes, and yes!!!!! He insisted that Anthony Q tell me that he's watching over me *all the time.* "I'm with her all the time," he said.

He talked about how he loved my food and that I am a good cook. Then he said that I made lasagna and cupcakes recently (I did! Those are not things I make very often anymore). He said they were good! He was able to taste them through me, I guess! I made gluten free cupcakes for a friend's wedding, and after several tries, they turned out really well. He said that people really liked them. And they did! Then he said I was a bit of a health nut (I'm vegetarian who eats gluten free and organic foods). Then Domenico stepped in and thanked me for taking such good care of his son (I was his nurse, his caretaker, his everything. I did Reiki energy work on him, etc.) Then Anthony Q laughed since they were both talking to him at the same time (that happened a lot in life). My Anthony said I took great care of him but that I feel like I could've done more (this is true). And he said I should stop feeling guilty and beating myself up (also true). He said that I did everything I could. I married him knowing he was sick but that I didn't care because I loved him so much (also true). Then he went on to describe my love of animals and how it would be dangerous for me to visit the Humane Society as I would want to bring them all home (very true)! "That's what a beautiful woman my wife is!" It brought such joy to hear him still referring to me as his wife!

Then my husband, through Anthony Q, gave me advice on how to handle some issues in my life. He talked about how I'm still grieving and still haven't gotten rid of many of his things. He mentioned his pillow (I sleep on his pillow). He mentioned his shoes (for fun, I wore his flip flops recently even though they are four sizes too big!). He was amused at that and said he loves that. Anthony Q then said, "Anthony told me that you also wear some of his socks!" I fessed up and mentioned, while laughing about it, that I sometimes wear his underwear!!!! He was a child at heart (me too) so he loved wearing superhero, South Park, Wolverine boxers. I kept some of these and recently started wearing them around the house as shorts/pajamas! We all laughed: Anthony Q, Domenico, Anthony, and I. We were all having a blast! My Anthony then explained how when I wear his clothes, sleep on his pillow, etc., it creates an instant connection with him. However, Anthony Q said that my Anthony is closer to me than his socks that I wear! That my Anthony was with me when I made the lasagna, when I made the cupcakes . . . he was with me *all of the time*!

I was amazed at Anthony Q's accuracy, but not surprised (if that makes any sense). It felt like I was talking directly to my Anthony. And Anthony Q is such an easy going, down-to-earth person that I felt very at ease and comfortable bringing up things such as my wearing my husband's underwear!

Then Anthony Q said that my Anthony was asking me to stop asking when we will be together again. "He wants me to tell you that it will be soon . . . , but not tomorrow. When it does happen, it will be like a blink of an eye, as though no time has passed since you last saw him."

"Anthony is telling me that you've given up but that you still need to live. You're still here because there're lessons you have yet to learn. He wants you to live but not for him."

Then Anthony Q asked me if I was thinking about writing a book. I had thought about it after Anthony died. I thought about writing about his life but then put it on the back burner. Then Anthony Q said, "He wants you to write the book. It's one of the things you are here to do—a book about healing. You're supposed to write something, he keeps insisting!"

Anthony Q continued, "He wants you to trust your abilities and believe in yourself. You don't trust! He says: *I believe in you!* He was your rock. **He Still Is**!!!" My Anthony would always be there to encourage me. Anthony Q said he's still doing it! "Please know he's okay. When you receive inspirations, write them down because they're coming from him! And then follow up on them."

Apparently some of the brilliant thoughts that I assumed I was having were from Anthony!

My Anthony told me through Anthony Q, "I will never die. My body died, but my love for you will never die." Then he thanked me for being there for him in his last moments and thanked me for telling him it was okay to go (I did). He talked about how I caressed his head before he passed.

And again Anthony Q said, "He wants me to tell you how much he loves you. I just don't have the words to tell you how much, he loves you beyond what any words can say. I love you for eternity. My love for you will never die. He just keeps saying, "I Love You, I Love You, I Love You, I Love You." He shows me how you two hugged all the time (we did, even in the grocery store aisles) and he's still hugging you," Anthony Q told me.

Again Anthony Q said, "I Love You, I Love You, I Love You, I Love You! He cannot say it enough and the hug doesn't end. He knows you miss his hugs and he's still hugging you."

Then I remembered something. A few weeks back I was going through a box of old papers and tossing them away. There was so much I was just grabbing handfuls of papers and throwing them out. Then I heard a voice in my head say, "Don't go so fast. There's something in there that you won't want to throw out." So I slowed down. Sure enough, a few pieces of paper later, I found the last card he ever gave me. It had a picture of the soles of feet of a little boy and a little girl and inside it said, "Sole mates from the start, Happy Anniversary."

Then he wrote "I Love You, I Love You. Love, Anthony"

Anthony Q was floored by this! He explained that he thought that Anthony was at a loss for words to express his love for me, and that is why he kept saying, "I Love You, I Love You, I Love You, I Love You" . . . but I knew he was referring to the card! This was another instance through which he wanted to show me that even if I don't feel him or hear him, *He Is Always There with Me*! Then Anthony Q said, "He's saying, 'please know that I love you . . . I love you . . . I love you . . . I love you . . . with that, he and Domenico are gone." Anthony Q then quickly clarified, "They're gone from me but not from you!"

This reading did so much for me. It gave me renewed confidence that my Anthony, Domenico, and all my loved ones are still with me, regardless of whether I can hear them or not. Suddenly I no longer felt alone. And I now had a feeling of purpose again.

I knew that Anthony Q was going to help me find direction. I realized days later that I had made Anthony responsible for my happiness. Then when he was gone (at least in body), my world crumbled and I felt like I would never be able to be happy again. I realized that it is the love that I feel for myself that is what is important. I began to look for love from within rather than from others. In this way I would be honoring Anthony the most.

I recorded the reading and later was amazed that it was just over an hour long. There was so much information relayed to me constantly that it felt more like two hours. Anthony Q's gift is so precious; it has helped to turn my life around.

Sofia Pico-Ambrosio

Anthony's note—One of the criticisms I've heard is that the souls all seem to say the same thing—"I love you." My response is that no matter how often someone who loves you says it, does it mean any less because they said it before?

Tonight Sophia's husband kept insisting that I tell her he was saying, "I love you. I love you. I love you. I love you." So I did.

"He loves you beyond words," I told her, trying to explain why I kept repeating this message to her. No other explanation was necessary. She knew why he kept saying it.

"A few days ago I was throwing away papers of his and I found a card from him. When I opened it, it had the most beautiful message. He had written over, and over again, 'I love you . . . I love you . . . I love you . . . I love you . . . '"

I was floored. So was Sophia. What a great way to let his wife know it was really him.

What a great message for *all* of us from the souls of our loved ones in the hereafter. "I love you . . . I love you . . . I love you . . . I love you. My physical life ended . . . my love for you *never* will."

Introduction

On Labor Day 2009, I was at a small gathering, sitting at a picnic table when a woman sat down in front of me. We introduced ourselves, and she asked what I did for a living.

"I'm a psychic medium," I told her. Her expression was blank, so I asked "Do you know what that is?"

She nodded. "Are you famous?" she asked me.

"Well, I'm internationally acclaimed," I said. "Does that count?"

She shrugged her shoulders, got up from the table, and walked away.

That night, as I lay in bed, I wondered, "Why aren't I more well-known?"

In all honesty, fame wasn't something I cared about. In fact, I was perfectly comfortable flying under the radar. I had built a good reputation for myself as a medium, and most of the people who came to me for readings were referred to me. I had done readings for people from Asia, Europe, the British Isles, Canada, Australia, and of course, the United States.

Still, her question, "Are you famous?" kept going through my mind. "If I did decide to come out from 'behind the curtain,'" I said to myself, "I'd do it by writing a book."

Let us fast forward to March 2010. I was contacted by a woman named Denise who told me she had heard good things about me from a friend of hers. She wanted to hire me to do a reading. As usual, she didn't tell me whom she wanted to hear from, and I didn't want to know.

The soul who came through for her and her family the night of the reading was Denise's daughter Jasmine, who had taken her own life on Christmas Day 2009.

Three weeks after Denise's reading I was awakened from a sound sleep. "What the . . . ?" I thought as I looked around my bedroom. "Oh, hi, Jasmine," I said silently so as not to wake up Cheryl, my girlfriend at the time.

"You have to write a book," Jasmine told me.

"Jasmine . . . honey . . . it's . . . ," I looked at the clock next to me, "3:30 in the morning. Can this wait until I wake up around 7?"

"No, you have to write a book for my mom, and everyone who is grieving," Jasmine insisted.

"Jasmine, I promise I'll get started on it after I wake up . . . "

"You've been thinking about writing a book for years . . . " It's true. I had talked about writing a book for years. I just didn't want to write a book about mediumship. I had received my certification in Spiritual Direction in 1999 from the Mercy Center in Colorado Springs, Colorado. I thought I'd write a book about spirituality, which I defined as "bringing spirit into reality."

"I don't know what I'd write," I protested.

"This is what your book can look like," Jasmine responded. I saw a vision of Elisabeth Kübler-Ross' book, a series of essays entitled *Life after Death*.

"I can do this," I thought as I got out of bed.

For the next two weeks Jasmine was my constant companion, encouraging me as I wrote my book, suggesting chapter subjects, and how to arrange my book.

"Okay, Jasmine, this was your idea, now I need you to help me find a publisher."

I submitted my manuscript to five traditional publishers. One of them I never heard back from. I received two rejection notices, and two expressed an interest in publishing my book. I decided to go with 4th Dimension Press, an imprint of the A.R.E. Press (the Association for Research and Enlightenment Press).

People assumed that because I was a published author, I was making more money than I could spend. Nothing could have been further from the truth, even though my book was selling around the world. I often spent hours, late at night or early in the morning, talking people "off of the ledge" without being paid for my time or asking to be paid, but still being accused of "profiteering" off of the grieving. I found my savings dwindling to the point where I had no money put aside at all.

Then the day came when every penny I had was gone. I was afraid. I didn't know how I was going to pay my rent and bills, let alone how I was going to buy food to eat. I became angry and resentful against the souls and the Eternal Light of Love. I went out one day to try to find a "real" job, but heard the souls insist that it wasn't what I was supposed to be doing.

"What do you want from me?" became my daily prayer. I found myself reexamining my life, my "gift," and the question of whether or not I wanted to continue doing the work. *More than once*, I told myself and God that I was done doing the work, only to make myself available to anyone who wanted a reading. If someone honestly couldn't manage to pay for a reading, I'd waive my fee, even if it meant that by doing so, I couldn't afford to buy groceries to feed myself.

Looking back, I see now that what God and the souls wanted was my attention. I had my own ideas of how my life would progress, and it wasn't until I finally gave up on the idea of living my life the way I wanted to live that I was able to understand that the time had come for me to move beyond being a "medium" to becoming *a teacher*.

The souls not only needed me to rethink my life, but they also needed to make me a better listener to what they were saying. What the souls wanted to tell me, and I wouldn't hear, was that the readings I had been doing were now meant for a greater purpose. I couldn't just be a bystander passing along the messages I heard only to their loved ones. I needed to pay attention to what was being said so that I could pass them along in a way that was much more far-reaching than to just those who were sitting in a session with me.

They wanted me to share what they had to say, teaching and creating hope in the hearts of *anyone* who was willing to listen. They wanted me to expand my vision of the work I was doing and my place in it so that I would to realize that they weren't just communicating with their loved ones anymore—they were communicating to everyone on earth who would listen to their wisdom.

The souls were telling me that the time had come for me to write this book and then created the events that made it possible for me to do so.

While the souls cannot tell us how to live our lives, they do their best to guide us, and inspire us, to make the journey while we're here a little more significant and prolific, empowering us to reap the rewards we can earn in the hereafter for doing so when our life here is over.

They want us to know that they haven't abandoned or forgotten us. They're here to help us whenever we truly need them.

I've learned a great deal while being privileged to be a part of sessions I've eavesdropped on as the souls share messages to their loved ones here. What I've heard has helped me not to fear the ending of my life or the lives of my loved ones.

The souls want to assure us that when the time comes for our loved ones and for us to crossover, there is nothing to worry about. They often talk about where they live, and where we will live, when it's our time. They talk about how happy and peaceful everything is in the hereafter. They work very hard to bring a three-dimensional reality to a world we can't yet see.

What you are about to read comes from the Eternal Light of Love through the souls. I cannot take any credit for some of the incredible things the souls want you to know about the life that waits for you when your journey here on earth is done. The material in this book is strictly from the souls and from what I learned when I finally started paying attention to what they were saying during the sessions they sent my way. If I wrote something contrary to what they wanted me to say, I'd find myself deleting sentences, paragraphs, and even chapters, and rewriting them until I was conveying the messages they need us to know while here on earth.

The souls insisted that this book contain real questions from real people. Let me reiterate that the replies to these questions aren't my responses. Whenever I was asked a question, I would typically go for a walk and listen to what the souls had to say. And talk they did.

My hope, and the hope of the souls, is that those who read this book will also know that there is nothing to fear—nothing at all! We are never alone on this journey back home.

Anthony Quinata
April 30, 2014

CHAPTER

1

What My Father Saw

On Thanksgiving Day 2009, my sisters Meridith and Nadine went to Saint John of God's assisted living facility in Los Angeles, California, where both my mother Rosalia and my father Antonio were in the hospital unit on the grounds. My father was there having suffered a heart attack the week before. My mother was there because she had broken her ankle. Because she suffering from moderate Alzheimer's, she couldn't understand why she was in a cast and confined to a wheelchair. My sisters were there to bring them food that was typically cooked on the island of Guam to celebrate the holiday.

Nadine went to my father's room to let him know that Meridith was getting my mother from her room so that they could enjoy a meal together. While she was talking to my father, she noticed that he wasn't paying attention to her but looking off to the right at the ceiling. "What are you looking at, Dad?" she asked him.

Our father looked at her and said, "I've been there before, baby. I

don't know when . . . I don't know how . . . but I've been there before."
He turned his attention back to the ceiling and something Nadine
couldn't see.

"Where have you been before, Dad? What do you see?" Nadine
asked, worried that he was hallucinating. "Dad, what is my name?
What day is today? How many children do you have?"

My father turned his attention back to her and said, "Deena, I'm
okay." With that he again looked away from her and up at the ceiling.
Meridith wheeled my mother in, and they all ate dinner together. My
father put aside his dessert, saying he would eat it later.

The next morning at 4 a.m. a nurse checked in on my father and
saw that he was sound asleep.

At 6 a.m. when he was checked on again, he had passed away.

Nadine told me this story the day before his funeral. "What do you
think he saw?" she asked me.

"Home."

CHAPTER

2

There Is More Than This

*L*ong before my father made his transition from this life to the hereafter . . . long before Angel told me that I myself had died, crossed over, and come back with knowledge to share with the world . . . long before Rick told me that my time as a medium was coming to an end so I could teach what the souls have taught me, I was standing on the sidewalk of a shopping center . . . and weeping—in front of God and anyone who happened to be walking by.

I was thinking about my friend, Camille, whom I loved, then and now. I was thinking about my family, my mother and father, and my brothers and sisters. And I was wondering what happened after life ended.

I remember praying to Christ, "You'd better not have been lying! I don't care about myself, but there had better be something more than this. If there isn't, then what's the point? Why do we love one another? We could just procreate like animals . . . " I don't remember what I said

3

after that. All I remember was that I grieving for those I loved who hadn't even died. I was grieving the idea of dying and never seeing them again. More than that, I was grieving the thought that good people who died ceased to exist. They deserved better than that, I thought to myself. Otherwise, nothing we do really matters, and this thing we call "life" is little more than a cruel joke.

Looking back I now believe that this was the day I was chosen to do the work that I do today—to act as a bridge between this life and the hereafter and to share the message with anyone who'll listen that death is not the end of life, love, or relationships . . . but a new beginning.

Although I didn't talk about it in my first book, there were several incidents that hinted at my ability. Like the time I worked for a company that sold burglar and fire alarms to homeowners. One night I was in the home of a woman who told me that she lived alone with her two children and wanted a system so they would feel safe. Halfway through my sales presentation I started bawling my eyes out, uncontrollably. She looked at me like I had lost my mind. I wondered if I had.

"Why are you crying?" she wanted to know.

"I don't know," I told her. "I just feel really sad all of a sudden, and I have no idea why!" I kept trying to compose myself, but I just couldn't. "Who died?" I blurted out suddenly.

The woman whom I was talking to looked at me shocked. "What are you talking about? No one died."

"Yes. Someone died . . . here . . . in this home." I insisted, having absolutely no idea where this was coming from. Then, suddenly, I did know. "It was your husband. He died. In this home. Around a month ago. That's why you want this system.

I have to tell you, he's still here . . . with you."

"How do you know that? How did you know my husband died here . . . a month ago?" she demanded, looking more than a little afraid of me.

"I don't know," I told her. "It just came to me."

With that she asked me to leave.

I went to see my friend Mary's new home before we went to lunch. I say "new" because she had just purchased it. While we were eating lunch, I said to her, "Did you know your home has a ghost?"

"Oh yeah," she said. "That's one of the reasons I wanted you to come and see it!"

How did I know it was haunted? It was a feeling I had. It was the same feeling I got when I would take a shower on Guam and felt like I was stepping out of the tub into a freezer. It was a chill I felt that wasn't external, but internal. It was the feeling I received whenever I was in the presence of a spirit that hadn't crossed over.

After lunch we went back to her house, and I had to use her bathroom downstairs. When I was done, I could hear her talking but couldn't find her. It took me a moment to realize she was upstairs. I started walking up to the second floor of her home and became aware of a young boy, around twelve, standing at the top of the stairs, wanting to know who I was and if I was Mary's boyfriend. When I told him she had invited me over to meet him, he offered to show me his bedroom which had nothing but boxes in it.

It turned out that Mary was in her upstairs bathroom and was talking on the phone. The young boy told me, "She does that a lot." When she came out of the bathroom, Mary found me halfway in a small storage space in the bedroom.

"What are you doing in there?" she asked, laughing.

"Your roommate is a young boy," I told her.

"I know," she said, which stunned me. "I see him a lot. I didn't tell you that because I wanted to see if you would pick that up."

"He told me that this is where he liked to play." I told her.

"What's his name?" she asked me.

"How should I know?" I asked back.

"Ask him!" she said.

It had never occurred to me to do any such thing in *all* of the investigations I had done up to that point. That was something the psychics I brought on the cases with me did, and I *wasn't* a psychic as far as I was concerned. But I asked anyway.

"His name is Michael. Now he says it's Scott."

"Which one is it?" I asked in my mind.

"He's saying his name is Michael Scott, but he liked being called Scott more than Michael." I saw a picture of a man wearing an officer's uniform that looked like it was from World War I. "His father was an officer in World War I," I continued.

I passed on several of the impressions I was receiving, such as the idea that he loved electronics and liked "to mess with your radio."

"I woke one night and the radio was on in my room. I knew I turned it off before I fell asleep, but it was back on and going up and down the dial. I told him to knock it off; I was trying to sleep," Mary said, laughing. "How did he die? And why, at such a young age?"

Again, I continued to pass on the impressions I was getting to her questions. "His lungs . . . something was wrong with his lungs. He says that they were black . . . he had a hard time breathing. His bed was right here near this window, and he liked to look out at the tree when he was sick."

And so it went that afternoon, but I wasn't taking much of it seriously because I thought that none of what I was saying could be verified . . . until we went back downstairs. We were walking through Mary's dining room, and I said, "Scott is telling me that this was the kitchen when he lived here."

"This was the kitchen for years until the owners I bought the house from remodeled it and made the patio area the kitchen."

"Scott says there was a pantry here." I said.

"There was until they remodeled. Part of the pantry is still here, but the other part they converted into the bathroom you were using." Mary confirmed, hardly fazed by what I was saying. To her, it was her friend Anthony being a psychic.

About thirty minutes after I left that afternoon, a woman named Chris came to cleanse Mary's home by burning sage. Mary told her to go on upstairs and do her thing. When Chris came down forty-five minutes later, she said to Mary, "Did you know that there's a young boy upstairs who died from tuberculosis and used to lie in bed in his room looking out the window at the tree you have in your backyard?"

"Oh yeah," Mary said, nonchalantly. "Anthony just told me."

It was after that day when my friend Sarah died in a freak car accident. At her memorial service my friend Cheryl suggested to me that my "thing" was talking to dead people.

I didn't consider myself to be a medium at that time. I didn't even know what a "medium" was. Looking back on it, I see that I was like an alcoholic who firmly denied the idea that he's a drunk.

CHAPTER

3

Don't Call Me a Psychic

At the time that all of this happened at Mary's house, if you would have asked me whether or not I was a psychic, I would have said, "No." I didn't consider myself to be a "psychic," highly intuitive, yes, but definitely not a psychic.

Now I know I was halfway correct. A psychic is someone with a highly developed sense of intuition and who can feel, intuitively, circumstances or information about the person he's "reading," or their loved ones, depending on the type of intuition the psychic has developed. That intuition may even let the psychic know circumstances of loss or future events around the person he's reading.

True mediumship, however, is something different altogether. For a medium, two elements have to be in place—a soul in the hereafter who wants to communicate and someone here who is willing to receive the messages. In other words, while psychics rely on their intuition to supply what they are passing along to their clients, mediums rely on communication from souls that have made the journey from this life to the next for the information they pass on. For short periods of time a medium can act as a bridge between this life and the next, linking the souls in the hereafter with their loved ones here and providing a human voice to the souls so that their messages can be communicated to those who otherwise couldn't hear or feel them.

I consider myself to be a medium. When I'm doing a session for a loved one(s), unless the information comes from the souls in the hereafter, I won't know it, and I don't have anything to say unless the messages come from the souls themselves.

When it comes to passing these communications along, I'm not perfect and I have never claimed to be. When it comes to understanding what I'm hearing, as anyone who knows me will tell you, I often get it wrong with those who are still living. Messages from the souls can, and do, get misinterpreted by me.

People think that I, as a medium, "talk to dead people." Actually, the exact opposite is true. They communicate with me. I listen and convey what I'm receiving to the members of their families who are still here. Whenever I'm doing a session, whether it's one-on-one, either in person or over the phone, a small number of people related to one another, or a small group of up to twenty-five, most of whom are strangers to one another, I always tell people to keep their answers to the evidence I'm giving to either "yes" or "no." I want only the absolute minimum information to let me know if I'm interpreting the evidence I'm receiving correctly or not. I say to people, "Most of what I'm telling you won't make sense to me, and it's not supposed to. This is not about me. It's about you. As long as the evidence I'm giving you makes sense to *you*, that's all I care about."

The messages in each session I do are like pieces of a puzzle that eventually come together into a solid picture. While no two sessions are the same, there is a distinct pattern that they follow starting out with general information, becoming more specific, and usually ending with a fact, name, or event that is known only to the soul and its loved one.

So what's the point? They want us to know that death is not a wall that separates us from them but a door between this life and the next and that their lives and the world they live in there are real.

CHAPTER

4

God Isn't the "Angel of Death"

The first time Flavio cut my hair, I did something I normally don't do—I brought through his sister, mother, and grandmother while he was cutting my hair. I deserved the haircut I received from him that day. In other words, it wasn't a good one. I freaked the poor guy out! Knowing that, I decided to give him another chance at cutting my hair, this time without the messages from his loved ones.

He told me during the second appointment that he had been praying to receive some kind of sign from God that his loved ones were okay, and he confirmed that his prayers were answered that day. He also told me that he had found a reason to live and be happy again. On June 17th, less than four months later, he passed away from a brain aneurysm.

One of my aunts passed from a long battle with cancer. As you might well imagine, I fielded a lot of questions regarding why people die when they do.

"Why did Flavio, who was so young and full of life, have to die so early? Why did God do this to him?"

One of my aunts posted on Facebook that her heart was breaking as she struggled with the question as to why God would take away another one of her sisters (my own mother being one of them). I have read other posts in groups I belong to on Facebook talking about "the day God took my (loved one) away," and the anger and confusion they feel towards God for doing so.

Several years ago I did a session in which a woman's mother came through telling her she needed to start grieving and start moving through her grief. Otherwise she'd never live the life God intended for her. The woman kept telling me that she was at peace that God took her mother away from her when she was only seven years old. "It was God's will after all."

"Really?" I asked her. "Do you think that God is the 'angel of death,' or that He was so bored that in order to amuse himself he thought he'd take away the mother of a seven year old, altering your life forever?" She thought about it for a moment, put her head in her hands and broke down, releasing a flood of tears that she had been keeping in for more than thirty years.

After my aunt's funeral I asked her sister, "Do you really think that God is the 'angel of death' and that he 'took' your sister from you?"

"No," she said, "I was angry and hurt and looking for someone to blame, but I don't believe that anymore."

The souls have assured me and want you to know that when it's time to move from this life to the next, the timing is always perfect. We may not understand the whys and wherefores now when we lose someone we love, but they say that after we've learned all of the lessons we're supposed to learn while we're here, our passing is a graduation from this life to life in a world of peace and bliss—a reward for job well done.

CHAPTER

5

A Party in Her Honor

A woman named Ann was dying from breast cancer. I was asked if I would offer a session as part of the silent auction that was being held at a benefit to help pay for her medical bills. "I'll go one further," I said, "I'll do a session for her. That way she'll know what to expect when her time comes. Hopefully, it'll help her."

The people who approached me told me that they loved the idea but weren't sure that Ann would agree because "she didn't believe in that sort of thing." Honestly, I wasn't surprised when she did agree to the session. It seemed perfectly reasonable to me that when Ann, or anyone else for that matter, comes to the point that she understands that physical death is inevitable, curiosity sets in as to what may be waiting when that moment finally arrives.

When I do a session for people who are terminally ill, it's not un-usual for them to hear from a number of souls of their loved ones who seem to be gathering during the session *en masse*, hoping to help them make their transition easier. In Ann's case however, it was only her aunt who showed up.

"She's telling me that there's a party being held in your honor in about three weeks," I told her.

Ann looked puzzled. "I don't know of any party. The only one I know of is that one tonight."

Her aunt repeated herself that there was going to be a huge party in Ann's honor three weeks from the day we were meeting. Ann looked at me and shrugged.

Twenty-two days later she was surrounded by her mother, her father, and her sister Mary when she drew her last breath. At her memorial, her father, unaware of the session between Ann and me, said that during the last three weeks of her life, Ann was more peaceful than he had ever seen her.

Terminal illness is a harsh way for life to end, not just for those who are dying but for those left behind. Standing by powerless, sitting and watching our loved ones fading, helpless to stop what can't be stopped, is difficult and puts a huge burden on our own souls. Watching the ones we love in so much pain leaves a lasting effect on us long after they're gone, and we're left here to grieve their absence. It tends to cause us to lose hope in the here and now and in the reality of the hereafter. We also lose a great deal of our loved ones before they're even gone.

But once they do succeed in moving from this life to the next, these souls insist that it's what they went through that was necessary and that they would gladly go through it all again to gain the same reward in the next life. Most of the souls I've heard from who have passed from cancer, or another terminal disease, often refuse to acknowledge any suffering they experienced because they've gained so much from it in terms of peace and joy in the hereafter. If they do acknowledge going through a rough time before their passing, it comes across as a distant memory, and they insist that not only did it end at the moment of their death, but it was also a valuable part of the new life they built for themselves in the hereafter.

CHAPTER

6

But I'm Not Dead

*L*isa told me about a dream she had involving her mother who had passed away just two months before.

"In my dream I was joking with her as I always did. She was directing me to do something as she always did. Anyway, my comeback to her telling me what to do in my dream was, 'Mom, I might listen to you . . . if *someone* didn't go and die.'"

What she said back to me was serious, but she seemed to be quite confused at the same time. "You're right, but I'm not dead . . . " Then she shook her head and said, "Well, I am dead . . . " then quickly added, " . . . I can't explain it."

Death comes for us all sooner or later. According to the U.S. Census Bureau someone dies in the United States every twelve seconds. Or do they?

Before I came to grips with my ability as a medium, or even knew what one was, I wore a T-shirt that said, "It's not that life is so short, it's just that death is so long!" Now I know better. According to the souls I've heard from over the years that I've been doing this work, the journey from this world to the next is as easy as walking from one room into another. Many of them have said that the transition is so subtle that it was hardly noticeable at all!

Others, whose passing came without warning, have talked about their passing being so low-key that it didn't occur to them that they were in the hereafter. I did a session in which a young man who had died in a car accident came through to talk to his parents. He said his first thought when he crashed the car was, "Mom is going to be pissed. She's going to kill me!" When I relayed that to his parents, his mother told me that he had totaled his car just the week before. She loaned him her car to go to work and told him, "You'd *better* not wreck my car if you know what's good for you!"

I've also heard from souls who said that, because of what they had been taught about what happens after we die, they thought the transition would be more obvious than it was. They were expecting a blinding light, angels, and saints heralding their arrival or demons pulling at their souls; but it wasn't like that at all. They were surprised to find out that they had "died" and that it didn't occur to them what had happened until *after* they saw loved ones, friends, and even pets, waiting to greet and welcome them back home. They talk about this happy "reunion" with a great deal of joy, seeing their loved ones that they thought they had "lost" to death.

And there are those souls who weren't surprised at their passing. They even welcomed it. My mother Rosalia, who passed a year and a half after my father and wanted more than anything to be with him again, came to me shortly after she drew her last breath and compared her transition to taking wet, heavy clothing off. She talked about the relief that came with the transition and the joy of being reunited with my father.

Others, like my father, are comforted by a glimpse of their life to come in the hereafter and the souls of their loved ones who had gone before them, before they actually leave the earth. Elisabeth Kübler-Ross and Dianne Arcangel, among others, have researched these "deathbed apparitions." Carla Wills-Brandon calls these visions "heavenly hugs."

CHAPTER

7

Death Is Not the End

*W*hile the souls all talk about essentially the same events, they describe the transition as being individual to them and what best suits their needs to make the transition from this life to the next easier on them.

The one consistent thing that all of the souls have said when they have talked about the moment of their physical death is a moment of darkness followed by seeing a entranceway open before them and that on the other side of that entrance they feel the peace and love that comes from it. They're irresistibly drawn to it like a moth to a flame. They move towards it because it just feels like the right thing to do. Even though they know that moving through this portal would mean the end of their physical life, they know that they're safe and secure, and it's the beginning of a new and glorious life.

They often say that on the other side of the entryway are their loved ones and even their pets, waiting to welcome them home. The souls consistently say that once they have crossed that threshold, they don't feel any need or desire to look back on the world they've left behind. They're happy to be moving forward into this place with its peace, love, and beauty beyond our wildest imaginings—an existence that defies anything that we could have made-up for ourselves during our life here.

CHAPTER
8

How Far Is Heaven?

What is the hereafter like?

First and foremost, it's a place where we receive a far-reaching appreciation for our life here on earth and for everything that happened during our stay here; it provides an understanding of why things happened the way they did and the peace of mind that comes with this understanding. All of our questions about ourselves are answered, including the life we lived while we were here on earth and the world we lived in. Questions, which we thought could not possibly have a resolution, are completely answered and in a way that allows us to fully understand our lives and the issues we faced during this time: the hurts, frustrations, and failings. We not only learn why our life was so difficult, but also what was the value and lesson contained in each one of our difficulties and how those difficulties helped us with our spiritual growth.

I clearly remember the day when the souls told me that our life in the hereafter will be a reflection of our life here. We are not bodies with a soul; we are souls with a body. We come here taking on a spiritual journey that will test who we are with struggles, lessons, and the circumstances we find ourselves in. Our ability to love ourselves and others, our compassion, and our willingness to make the world a better place, will be put to the test. How well we live up to these ideals will, according to the souls, create the kind of home we experience in the hereafter.

On the other hand, if we fall short on any of these ideals we brought with us to earth and behave poorly while we're here, we create the conditions in the hereafter in which we'll continue to learn and grow, once our time here on earth is over.

That's why answering the question "What is the hereafter like?" can be as difficult as explaining the color green to someone who has been blind since birth. The afterlife is what we create it to be, based on the lessons we have learned, or didn't learn, while we were here on earth. This is also why the souls want you to know exactly why you're *here*.

You are here on earth to go on a journey through this life for a specific period of time, which may be as long as a hundred years or as short as a few minutes or hours. You come here knowing that you will go through a series of ups and downs, highs and lows, joys and sorrows, all of which were planned by you before you came. The souls say you do this so that you may learn a specific lesson which will allow you to advance spiritually in order to experience more fully the beautiful world that is your reward for having lived here.

It might surprise you, as it did me, to hear that life in the hereafter is surprisingly like life here, but with important differences. The problems we faced here no longer exist— no one dies young and no one grows old. No one suffers or becomes sick. No one feels lonely or frustrated with themselves or those around them.

What is similar is that, according to the souls, the world you find yourself in will look a lot like the one you left here. You'll see people, places, and things that you'll recognize from your life here, but with one important difference—joy and love will saturate everything you touch, everything you see, and everyone around you.

The souls say that they live in communities with friends and loved ones they knew here on earth and thought they had lost. They spend their time doing things that make them happy, bring them joy, and make them feel complete. They also do what they can to help bring about joy and peace to others, especially those they love who are still here.

In their world there is no pain, no anger, no regret, or no feelings of shame. Their sense of who they are, especially in the eyes of the Eternal Light of Love, and their sense of happiness is beyond anything they ever felt while they were here on earth.

While we on earth may call it Heaven, Paradise, or Nirvana, to the souls who live there, it is the Other Side of this life, where they are reaping the rewards of their struggles while they were here on earth—to them, it's *home*.

How far is Heaven?

Anthony,

I would like to know exactly where the afterlife takes place. We look to the heavens in prayer, so is the afterlife high up past the clouds and sky? I thought about that last year on a flight to Europe.

We hear of different dimensions and realms, but what are they? When people pass on, do they step out of their bodies and through a door that opens only at death?

It is hard to wrap my mind around these issues, but maybe this is where faith comes into play. We know that there is life after death but where it takes place is a secret of sorts. We have faith in God, but what he looks like is a mystery to us mortals. Does any of this make sense? I have not been blessed with any gifts of communication with departed souls.

I do know that I can talk to my departed loved ones, but I wonder if they hear me because I can't hear them answer back in words. I don't know about signs. People find feathers and so do I, but couldn't they be from birds that have flown over?

If our loved ones can see us, why can't we see them? What exactly divides us?

Barb

I love these questions! In all honesty, I could and have talked for a couple of hours answering questions like this in seminars, but I'll (try to at least) be brief!

I would like to know exactly where the afterlife takes place.

There's a story about a fish who heard of something called "water." This fish became obsessed with finding out where this thing call "water" was, so it asked other fish about it. The other fish admitted they didn't know where to find "water," but one of them suggested he ask the wise old fish for an answer.

So the fish went to the wisest fish in the ocean and said, "I've heard of this thing called 'water' and I was told you can tell me where I can find it."

The wise old fish looked at him and laughed.

When night falls, what happens to the daylight? Where does it go? Light and darkness are the same energy, but light vibrates at a much higher rate.

Life on the Other Side vibrates at a much higher rate than here. That's why we can't see it, even though it's all around us. We walk around in the dark, thinking what we can see is all there is to see.

We are enclosed by the love of God, according to the souls, the way fish are surrounded by water. One of the reasons we aren't aware of this is because we believe that we're separate from God. It's this feeling of separation that caused us to want to come here to begin with— to learn that we're not separate from God at all.

These lessons are learned in myriad of ways: the joys, triumphs, trials, and difficulties of our lives; in the people we love and who love us; and in those whom we hurt and who hurt us.

We look to the heavens in prayer, so is the afterlife high up past the clouds and sky?

"Two men looked out from prison bars,
One saw mud, the other saw stars."
                                                    Anonymous

We look to the "heavens" when we pray because it represents us looking up with hope and faith, especially when we're feeling down. The souls constantly say that they're not in some place far away, but that they're closer to us on the Other Side than they ever could have been while they were here.

We hear of different dimensions and realms, but what are they?

When the souls speak of "dimensions," think of different grades in school. Each grade represents what we've learned, what we are learning, and what we can learn. Ultimately, some of the souls earn their PhDs which represents complete union with the Eternal Light of Love. They are "one with God."

When people pass on, do they step out of their bodies and through a door that opens only at death?

Shortly after my own mother passed, she compared giving up her physical body at the moment of death to shedding wet, heavy clothing. She talked about feeling a freedom that made death a relief.

The souls also say that death is as simple as walking out of one room and into another. They say that whatever fears we have about dying are completely unfounded.

That doesn't mean they walk through a door or enter through "Pearly Gates" however. The transition is so subtle that many souls have told me they're surprised they "died" to begin with. They talk about transitioning from this life to an even "greater life," but not realizing it until they see loved ones who have gone before them.

I know that I can talk to my departed loved ones and wonder if they hear me because I can't hear them answer back in words. I don't know about signs. People find feathers and so do I, but couldn't they be from birds that have flown over?

Many people think that when I'm reconnecting their loved ones with them during a medium session that I'm having a conversation with them. I wish it were that simple! When I "hear" from them, they're communicating with me through feelings and emotions. It's the same way as they do with you.

Any "verbal" communication comes through as a thought. Except I normally don't think "I died from cancer." "Say, Natalie." or "I loved cooking and was good at it."

Another way they communicate with me is by showing me symbols. If I see candles, I know they are talking about prayers. If I see a car accident, it could mean that they died in a car accident, that they died accidentally, or that someone here was in an accident.

"Signs" such as feathers are physical ways that the souls communicate with you similarly to the ways that they communicate with me in my mind. Could the feather have fallen from a bird in the sky? Absolutely! But it's the soul inspiring you to think of it when you see the feather that makes it a "sign."

If our loved ones can see us, why can't we see them? What exactly divides us?

I cannot stress this enough. Nothing divides us from those we love on the Other Side.

As I said before, light and dark are the same energy—one just vibrates at a higher level than the other. It's the same with those of us still here and those who have gone on before us. Again, we believe in the illusion of separateness because we walk around in the dark thinking that what we can't see doesn't exist.

Those on the Other Side have the advantage of seeing "clearly" and want to help us because they can see what we can't.

What they want us to know is that there's a reason for everything which happens in our lives. It's to help us grow spiritually, by moving up a "grade" or two or three . . . when we return back home. Their hope is that by communicating with us through signs and mediums such as me, we won't give up hope, but will keep putting one foot in front of the other until we're reunited once again on the Other Side.

Where was Jesus?

Many years ago my grandmother was on the brink of death in the hospital. We were all sitting around her, and she began mumbling about seeing Heaven and her own mother and family on the Other Side. Someone asked her if she saw a certain family member and she didn't answer.

Then, I asked if she saw Jesus. (I was a strong believer and really wanted to know if she saw him). Everybody in the room whipped their heads around real fast and glared at me as if I had just asked an offensive question. My grandmother looked around confused, seeming as if she couldn't find him.

I never knew what to make of that experience, but it started me questioning . . . where was Jesus?

Why wasn't He there and why did she look so confused when I asked?
Andi

First of all, I want to say that your story illustrates something that the souls say all the time—no one makes the transition alone. Even souls who have told me they were either asleep, or in a comatose state when they crossed over, were aware of loved ones who had gone before them, joyfully waiting for and preparing them for their journey back home.

Can you imagine being brought up to believe that Jesus was going to judge you for your sins and might condemn you to "hell" for them; and then he's the *first* person you see when you cross over?

What if you were raised or converted to Buddhism? What if you were born into the Islamic tradition? Or Judaism?

That's why those we love, and who have loved us, are there to greet us, whether it's during a "death-bed vision" or after we cross over.

Children, especially young ones, who have no idea who their relatives are, are greeted by bunny rabbits, kittens, puppies, and other small animals according to the souls. After they become comfortable with these creatures and their unconditional love, they are then led to relatives such as grandparents, who welcome them back home.

Once the newly arrived soul adjusts to its new surroundings and existence, then "Christ" appears to the soul and may be seen as "Jesus" or "Buddha" or Muhammad," etc., depending upon the beliefs that the person had when he was alive.

Whomever the souls see, their experience is one of being **unconditionally loved** and accepted for who they are—and not as being judged.

So where was Jesus? He was waiting patiently, and lovingly, to welcome your grandmother back home, with a heart of love, eyes that understand and accept, and arms to hug her, saying, "I love you. I missed you. I'm so happy you're home. Now, share with me what you have learned."

Thus begins what the souls refer to as the "life review."

Is there such a thing as purgatory?

"Is there such a thing as purgatory? If so, how do souls get into Heaven?"
Vivian

When I've asked the souls about religion, they've compared the various faiths to facets of a diamond, saying that they all show an aspect of the truth, but none reflect ALL of the truth. That's the reason they refer to their existence in the hereafter as the "Other Side." Terms such as Heaven, Nirvana, Paradise, have a religious association that they want to avoid.

So when I asked them about "purgatory," I was told, "It does exist, but not in the way it's been taught."

Many times, when I've done a reading, I get the feeling from the souls that they're on a vacation that they were never able to take while they were here. I looked on Dictionary.com and here's one of its definitions of the word "vacation."

3. Freedom or release from duty, business, or activity.

Think of duty, business, or activity being our life here on earth.

They talk about life on the Other Side closely paralleling our life here but without the drama. Yet it does have all of the joy we missed out on while we were here. They also say that if there's something you didn't get to experience here, you can create the experience there as long as it's in line with the will of the Eternal Light of Love.

For example, if you lived in a shack here, dreaming of living in a mansion and feeling like you missed out on that when you return to the hereafter, they say you can create it simply by thinking of it there. Not only that, you'll be able to live in it until you "get it out of your system" and are ready to move on to more meaningful experiences.

If you've created havoc and hurt while you were here, you're given the opportunity to repair it from the Other Side as well.

Moving beyond these needs on the Other Side, "purging them" is what allows us to move forward on in our spiritual journey and closer to the Eternal Light of Love.

Do our loved ones hang around before moving on?

"Is it true that your love ones who pass hang around for only a certain time and then they have to move on to the next phase of their life?"
Wendy

I have to admit that when I first read your question, I wasn't sure I understood what you were asking. My first thought was to say that according to Mary Ann Winkowski, the woman who inspired the television show "The Ghost Whisperer," there is something like a seventy-two hour window during which a soul can choose to cross over to the Other Side. During those seventy-two hours, according to Winkowski, the spirits will check in on various loved ones, attend their own funeral to see what it was like, who showed up, who didn't, etc.

The problem is that this information totally flies against what the souls who have crossed over have told me, but then again, she freely admits to talking to "ghosts," not souls who have crossed over. So I decided to look at your question again, from the point of view of a medium who was trained "on the job" to do this work.

It sounds to me as though you're asking if the souls are with us for only a certain period of time before they have to move on and leave us here to fend for ourselves. If that's the case, then I can tell you that the answer is definitely "no!"

The souls have said that when they cross over, the last thing they are doing is "resting in peace." They are busy reaping the rewards that they deserve from the finishing the lessons they came here to learn and earning their transition from this life to a better world. They talk about doing work that is fulfilling to them and living their lives filled with peace, joy, and love in everything they touch, everything they see, and everyone they meet. What they haven't done is forget their own lives here and how difficult it was—not just for themselves, but their loved ones still here. Because of that they often talk about being closer to us in a way that wasn't possible while they were here on earth.

I've heard several souls, during sessions I've done, talk about the most common place things during readings. "Your husband is laughing at how you burned dinner last night," I told one woman. She was confused about why he would waste his time talking about that instead of more "sensible" things.

"He wants you to know that as busy as his life is there, he still sees you and is with you on the Other Side," I told her. "He's letting you know that he's never too busy to waste all of his time on you. Frankly, I can't think of anything more important he could say to you than that."

So my answer would be that while there is a period of time spent adjusting to their new life, once they've adjusted to being home in the hereafter, part of their life there includes "hanging around" us, helping as much as they can *without* interfering in our life's lessons, and guiding us when we go off course. They are never too busy or have moved so far away that they cannot answer our calls for help or give us the reassurance we need that they haven't abandoned or forgotten us.

I'm losing my home. Will I lose my son too?

I hope you can answer this for me. My home is being foreclosed on. Sell date is June 11. It is tearing me up. My seventeen-year-old son blossomed here.

Steven was taken from me on May 22, 2010, hit by a car while riding his bicycle. I am not sure I have seen him out of corner of my eye on several occasions or if it is wishful thinking. However, I am sure I feel him around me.

I cannot see any way to save our house. My fear is that once we move, his spirit won't be able to find me. Do our loved ones follow us if we are forced to move?
Virginia

First of all, I want to tell you I'm sorry to hear about the loss of your son. If that wasn't enough, your family is now about to lose the home your son grew up in. My heart goes out to you, and I'll keep you and your family in my daily prayers.

Now let me answer your question. My long, and short, answer to your question is, "YES!" It's not so much that your son will "follow" you wherever your family goes as he is *always* with you, *no matter where you are.*

I love the idea that you see him out of the corner of your eye on occasion and that you feel his love around you. In my opinion it's his way of letting you know that he wasn't "taken" from you. He's reaching out to you to show you that there's more to this lifetime than we can ever imagine and that you have reason to hope, no matter what struggles you're going through here on earth, including losing your home. That's why you'll never "lose" him, because he's there to be a beacon of hope, reassuring you that at the end of all of your struggles you'll be reunited with him in a world of peace.

Having said that, with all of the shows about "ghosts" on television and in the movies, I can see how you might be afraid that your son might get "stuck" in your home. The truth is that most of those shows are about entertaining you by playing on your fears and are not based in reality.

The reality is that your son isn't stuck anywhere. What happened to him might seem like an unfortunate accident, or God taking him away from you, but the truth is that he *earned* the transition from this life to the hereafter by completing his journey here so he could move onto a better world. And he's able, from that world, to be with you no matter where you end up in this phase of your journey here on earth.

CHAPTER
9

Pain Like No Other

*P*arents who have come to me to reconnect with their children who have died, especially if their child did so at a young age, often worry about their children being scared and alone at the time of their passing. From all of the readings I've done involving children, it seems that the Eternal Light of Love will create surroundings that children will understand and gravitate towards. For example, children will see someone like St. Nicholas or Santa Claus. It will be somebody who greets the children and who is immediately recognizable and attractive to children, no matter what their culture or religious beliefs and who introduces them to other children in a setting where they can play together.

Animals are a great anxiety reliever in the hereafter just as they are here. If children have had a family pet which passed on before them, that pet will meet them in the hereafter and guide them toward the Light. Fawns, puppies, kittens, and bunny rabbits are also used to comfort the soul of a child. They are soon greeted by and introduced to family members they may not have known while they were here but whom they will now live with and be cared for by on the Other Side. During many of the readings I've done, I've heard from grandparents, aunts, and uncles telling parents not to worry; they reassure them that their children are in good hands and will be well taken care of until the day that they're reunited once again. "After all, they're part of my family too!"

Why would someone choose to be a bereaved parent?

Anthony, I've read you and others saying that we choose the kind of life we're going to live while we're here to learn lessons. But why would I, or anyone else, choose to lose a child? Since my daughter died, I hurt so much and all I want to do is be with her.
Debbie

I've heard the souls repeatedly say that when we come into this life, we come here to learn lessons. When we've finished learning those lessons, we go back "home." They also say that the amount of time we're here is set and the only variable is the circumstances under which our passing happens.

Some of us come here with lessons that will require less time to learn or teach others, for that matter. Others come knowing that they'll be here much longer. Those who are coming here for a short time need someone who will be here for a longer period of time to make their journey here on earth possible. In other words, they need souls who will be parents to them and for whom the journey of "grieving parent" will enable them to learn the lessons they have come here to learn. Or teach.

I can't think of a better example of this than a woman named Karen, who was referred to me by one of my former clients. Her son J.P. started coming through as I was explaining to his mother what she could expect during the session.

"I don't know how else to say this," I told her, "but he stopped breathing. I know I'm stating the obvious here; when we pass, we stop breathing, but that's all he keeps saying, 'I stopped breathing.'"

Karen nodded her head that she understood. For my part, I kept asking her son what led to his passing and all I kept getting was, "I just stopped breathing." He also talked about his sister finding him, trying to give him CPR, and then calling their mother to tell her the tragic news.

I saw two cars crashing which means to me that the passing involved vehicles, as in a car accident, or that it was accidental. "J.P. is saying that his passing was an accident." Karen nodded.

I saw J.P. bringing the fingers of both of his hands to his chest. When I see this, the soul is telling me that his life ended by his own hand. "Your son took his own life . . . yes?" Karen shook her head, no. Now I was totally confused. "Well, he's telling me that you've made his passing a personal cause, and he's proud of you for doing so."

Karen nodded, with tears in her eyes. "That's true. I have," she said quietly.

I asked her son to give me something else I could tell his mother. "He's saying he had a very dry sense of humor." Karen nodded, smiling.

"He's telling me to compare my sense of humor to his," I told Karen. "I asked him how I'm supposed to do that, and he wants me to talk about my fart machine." I pointed to a black device that made gassy sounds when I pressed a remote control button. Why the machine was there next to her, I have no idea. I didn't remember putting it where it was or why I did it.

Up until this point, Karen honored my request that she keep her responses to the messages to "yes," or "no." But when I brought this up, Karen started laughing and said, "That is really meaningful to me. Do you want to hear why?"

"I'd love to hear it, if you want to share," I told her, grateful for the break in the intensity of the session.

"Just before I came here, I told J.P., 'If you're really the one coming through to me, I want you to say the word fart—not flatulence or gas but fart.' I'm always farting," she told me. "I'm a human fart machine!"

I couldn't help but laugh out loud with her. I also couldn't imagine this woman sitting in front of me being a "fart machine."

"You were also right when you said that my son simply stopped breathing and that's what caused him to die. You said that he was

saying he died 'at home.' He did, but not at my home. He died in his
grandmother's home. He suffered from anxiety attacks and asked his
grandmother if he could have one of her hydrocodone pills to help
him sleep. He drank a beer with it. That's what killed him.

Most people don't know something like this can happen, but someone dies every nineteen minutes this way. My husband and I have
started a foundation to help make people aware that this can happen."

What the particular lessons were that J.P. came here to learn weren't
something he shared with Karen. What he did do was to encourage
his mother to keep up what she was doing. That's why she came here.
That's why she was still here.

"Starting the foundation wasn't my idea; it was my husband's," Karen
told me. "I didn't want to have anything to do with it. I was too caught
up in my grief, so he started it on his own. After a while I knew that it
was something J.P. would have wanted me to do too, so I got involved."

Honestly, I'm convinced that the foundation which she and her
husband created after their son's death will save lives in the future.

For more information about the J.P. Prescription Drug Awareness
Foundation, please visit www.jpawarenessfoundation.org.

Are my babies still babies in Heaven?

*I have a question. I have thought about this for a long time, "Are my twins
still babies or do they grow in Heaven as here on earth?"*

*They would be turning three years old on January 24. It's one of my
unanswered questions.*
Twana

First of all, I want to say that I'm sorry for your loss and reassure
you that your children are safe and happy in the Heaven.

When a soul chooses to come to earth, it does so with a specific
lesson in mind. These lessons are designed not only for its spiritual
growth here, but for the rewards it will earn in the hereafter for having
gone through this time on earth. When the lesson is finished, no matter what age the soul is, it "graduates" and returns back home. Age is
not something that's taken into consideration as to when a person
passes from this world into the next as far as the souls are concerned,

only the amount of time it will take to finish its task and learn those lessons while it was here. As far as the hereafter is concerned, *there is no such thing as time.* No matter how long or short the period of time it was here, when it returns home to the Other Side, the souls say that the time they were gone is like a blink of an eye.

So the answer to your question is "No, your twin babies are not three years old in Heaven," but they are still your children and you are still their mother. They have grown in the sense that they returned to the Eternal Light of Love having learned the lessons they came here to learn and are now reaping the rewards for having done so.

Frankly, I love doing readings in which children come through because of their purity of thought and energy. They are so "alive" when they come through, and they want so desperately to comfort their parents and to let them know that they are okay. They know how much their parents are suffering so they want more than anything to make their parents feel better and to let them know that they are still with them.

Please know that the same is true of your babies.

Will my child know me in Heaven?

I lost my first daughter Wendy when she was eighteen months—a beautiful little girl who died in a tragic accident. My question is, "Will she know me though her life was short?"
Grant

You've expressed a concern that many bereaved parents I do readings for have . . . that their child will age on the Other Side and will be unrecognizable as "middle-aged" adults by the time they see them again. I've even heard other mediums make the same claim that children do age in the hereafter.

The truth is, according to the souls, the souls who passed as children, progress in wisdom and understanding of who they are, but that they don't "age." So when it's your time to return home and you see your daughter again, you will see her as she last appeared to you, and I'm sure you'll be able to hold her in your arms again the way you did when she was still here.

Keep in mind that we mark time while we're here, but to your daughter it'll be like a blink of an eye since she last saw you.

Why are some babies never born?

My twins would be twenty-seven now, but I had miscarried before they were ever born. How will we know each other when we reunite if we never saw each other? And why are some babies never born? Why do some women miscarry?
Jeanette

A miscarriage occurs when the body inside the womb of the mother is unable to be used as a vehicle necessary for the soul to fulfill a specific spiritual journey. The souls say that a physical body has life because a soul lives within it. When a soul recognizes a physical body that will be the perfect vehicle and that will give it the chance it needs to learn a specific lesson or lessons here on earth, it chooses to enter it. For reasons known only to a particular soul and which only that soul can understand, it may choose not to enter the body. Since the developing body cannot survive without a soul, the result is a miscarriage or a stillborn birth. In other words, it's exactly the same as a soul leaving a body at the end of its life here on earth.

Even so, the souls of miscarriages or stillborn children will appear to a family during a session (at least with me). They may or may not be recognized, but in the hereafter, they still consider themselves to be a son or daughter just as much as if the birth cycle had been completed. They were a part of the family talking to me and call their parents during the session "Mom" and "Dad."

Your twins are still your children, and you will see them when your time here is done.

He was eighteen years old here. Is he now a thirty year old in Heaven?

If people on the Other Side revert to their thirties, what happens to the people who died young? Will I meet my eighteen year old as he would have been in his thirties?

*Also, after you pass, you have lessons to learn and soul growth to achieve
. . . how exactly is this done?*

*Do they read and learn? Do they observe living loved ones and learn?
Do they become guardian angels?*
Sarah

Several years ago after I moved out of my parent's home, I still
stayed in touch with my family over the phone. I remember hearing
Steve's (my youngest brother) voice change during the time I was away.

When I came home to visit, I didn't see Steve at first, but after I was
unpacking and getting settled in my room, behind me I heard, "Hi,
Anthony." I recognized his voice, turned around, and was shocked to
see how much he had grown. I'm not sure I would have even recognized him if I hadn't heard his voice first.

In much the same way, souls don't recognize each other by their
physical appearance, but by the love they have for one another.

I've talked to a number of parents who are afraid that their young
child will be a "middle-aged" adult whom they won't recognize when
they're reunited in the hereafter. They talk about grieving the thought
of missing their child's development on the Other Side. I reassure them
that it's not an issue because what souls do not do is age, but grow
spiritually, because of the opportunities they had while they lived here
on earth.

There's no danger in not recognizing your child when you're reunited again. You will, in fact, see your son as you knew him because
your son will present himself to you in that way to help you adjust to
the idea that you've transitioned from this life to the next, and secondly, for the joy you will experience seeing him again in the hereafter. You'll also rejoice at the way he's matured spiritually because of
the time he was here on earth.

I can reassure you that what won't happen is that he'll greet you by
saying, "Hi, Mom," followed by your confusion at seeing a "total
stranger" standing in front of you. You'll know beyond a shadow of a
doubt it's your son standing before you, because of your love for him
and his love for you.

To answer the second part of your question, we come here to learn
because the lessons are easier to learn here. Why? Because we are

continually "tested" here by the difficulties we experience on earth. Our response here determines our life in the hereafter. The more we respond by growing in love, the greater our reward, according to the souls.

If someone responds to the hardships here by creating even more havoc and difficulty for him and others, that will be reflected back on him in his life on the Other Side. For that reason I've heard souls say, "I'm never doing that again. It was just too hard. I'll learn the lessons I need to learn here, even if it does take longer to do so here."

The souls who have come here say that we take the lessons that we learned here and apply them to our even greater life there. Everything here is a dim reflection of the Other Side. This is why we need to learn our lessons to the best of our ability while we're here. The life we create here is magnified many times over when we return.

The souls also say that part of their spiritual journey there is to assist us in ours here. In other words, it's perfectly okay to think of them as your "guardian angels." They continually assure their loved ones in sessions I've done that while they're not "resting in peace," they are never too busy to assist us when we need them. All we have to do is think of them.

10

This Is Your Life!

The souls say that once we enter into the hereafter, and before we journey to the Eternal Light of Love, we experience a clarity and understanding of why everything happened the way it did. They refer to this as the "life review."

The souls describe it as a movie in which all of our life's questions are answered. We finally begin to understand the point of everything we had to go through during our life here on earth. It shows how the struggles we went through served a certain purpose in order to bring about our spiritual growth, and it highlights what we need to learn as our journey continues on in the hereafter.

We see where we have stayed close to our life's purpose, thus accomplishing good. We are shown where we wandered away from our path and the purpose for our being here and how we could have done better. We see the impact that our life and actions had on those around us—from an objective and unbiased point of view.

The souls say that while God, or the Eternal Light of Love, is with us during our life review, it's not to judge us or what we did during our time here on earth. While it's easy for us to remember all of the awful things we had done to others, it's harder for us to summon up all of the good things we've done that deserve to be recognized. Fortunately, these are the very things that are never forgotten by the Eternal Light of Love.

So our life review is not a means used by God to judge how much punishment we deserve for the wrongs we did during our life on earth. Punishment doesn't exist in the hereafter in the way we think about it. The Eternal Light of Love doesn't make mistakes but understands when we do.

Each one of us will judge our own actions and decide what we need to do in the hereafter to repair the wrongs we have done. We will also learn the lessons we missed while we were here on earth. The lessons we didn't learn while we were here are continued in the next life so that we can move closer to and experience even more the Eternal Light of Love. The good news, according to the souls, is that during the life review, we come to understand that whatever damage we did, is reparable in the hereafter, due to the grace given to us by the Eternal Light of Love.

Once our life review is over, we'll have a clear understanding of the whys and wherefores of our life on earth. We will also know the spiritual work we'll do in order to continue our growth in the hereafter. We begin to release all of the troubles that bound us to this life on earth. We are shown the rewards we've earned, and all of the grief, struggles, and suffering we endured while we were here will start to become a distant memory.

Some of the souls want to share what they've learned with their loved ones still here on earth. Whenever people ask me why the souls in the hereafter would want to communicate with those they left behind, my standard answer was, and still is, love. They do so motivated by their love for us.

I've since learned that there's another reason. They do it because it brings them joy.

The souls talk about how they realized during their life review how much joy came from helping others while they were still here on earth.

Having lived a complete life here on earth and seeing the reasons for the ups and downs they experienced here during their life review, many of them want to share what they've learned to make the road a little smoother for anyone here who is willing to listen to them and take what they say to heart.

The souls seem to be no different from those of us still here who want to teach what we know—especially when we see someone struggling with the problems we have faced. Some of the souls who have come through during my sessions have told their loved ones that part of their spiritual growth in the hereafter is to guide those here on earth so that they can avoid the very same issues that kept these souls from learning their lessons while here on earth. Now that they've "been there and done that," it's much easier for them to see how we can get hung up here, by making bad choices and getting stuck on our own spiritual journey. What they have to say can serve us much the same way as signs on a highway that let us know where we are, how far we have to go, what detours are ahead, when to get off the road we're on, and when to go on a different road altogether to reach our destination.

The souls are prohibited by the Eternal Light of Love from interfering in our lives because it might take away from the lessons we are here to learn. That's why they can't force us to listen or follow their guidance, but they never give up trying to inspire us. It is their hope that what they say will provide some strength in our grief and angst, when we're feeling lost, alone, and unable to go on.

Finally they want to destroy the idea that death is the end of everything. They want you to know that when they leave this life, you are not being abandoned or punished. Your loved ones haven't left you at all, but are still with you, watching over you. Death is not the end of life, love, or relationships. It's a beginning.

Our life on earth is a small fragment of the journey we travel moving closer to the Eternal Light of Love. Life never ends and neither do we. We live forever. It's with this awareness that they reach out to their loved ones, and they speak to people like me, hoping to get across this powerful message of hope, love, and peace to whoever is willing to listen.

CHAPTER

11

I'm Sorry!

ew things get me going the way it once happened when I thought about what I had heard come out of the mouth of a woman from Texas whose reading I had just finished. She told me that she had seen another medium who told her that she needed to quit grieving the loss of her friend Jake because he was obnoxious and she was keeping him from "progressing" on the Other Side.

Every soul that crosses over finds itself in a place of beauty, serenity, and peace. It might have acquired beliefs and defenses in this life as a way of dealing with the harshness of this world, but on the Other Side there just isn't any need to act that way. When the soul sees the harm it caused in its relationships here due to its behavior, its desire is to repair whatever damage it has done. The soul knows this isn't going to happen by coming through and inflicting even more pain during a reading.

People, who hurt other people in this life, were often hurting themselves. When they cross over, the source of their pain no longer exists, and they're able to see what effect their behavior had on others, especially those who loved them.

I've been asked why someone in Heaven would want to come back here to talk to anyone he might have left behind. I tell them that the motivation is typically love. It's love that causes a soul, who may have hurt us by its actions, to want to come back to say, "I'm sorry." In all of the sessions I've done, there has never been a soul who came through saying, "Yeah, I was a jerk to you, but it was only because you were such a bitch to me!" There have been countless times when souls have come through saying, in essence, "I was an SOB to you. I'm sorry." No excuses, no reasons, and no justification for being the way they were in this life. And there's no reason for them to be "obnoxious" in the next.

What should probably have been "I was an ass" from this soul, came out as "I am an ass" from this "medium." In my opinion, if she really were communicating with Jake or any other soul in an authentic way, she would not have made this mistake. What ought to have been an opportunity for reconciliation became a source of pain.

Then, rubbing salt into her wounds, the "medium" told this woman to quit grieving because it was hindering Jake's progress on the Other Side! Really? Don't get me started . . . Okay, too late.

Grief is the price we pay for love. Grieving is another way of saying, "I love you." Unfortunately, what this woman did was try to keep a lid on her grief by, in essence, suppressing her love for her friend. Think about it. She was repressing her love out of love, and this caused her to grieve even more and to beat herself up for doing so.

When someone claiming to be a medium tells you that your grief is keeping your loved one from moving on in the Other Side, just know that this person is not getting that from a soul on the Other Side. If there's such a thing as grieving "too much," then the only progress being impeded might be yours, in *this* life.

The souls see this. They break through the veil that separates our worlds to let you know that they're okay, that they're not suffering, and that they haven't abandoned us. We are not alone, no matter how much it might feel that way. They do this so that, while we might not be able to stop grieving while we're here, we can at least move through our grief, living our lives knowing that one day we'll be reunited with those we loved.

Telling someone, as this "medium" told my sitter, to stop grieving is akin to saying, "Don't waste your love on someone you lost; you're keeping them from being happy."

What a load. Don't believe it.

Why do souls say they're sorry?

Why do loved ones always say "I'm Sorry" in messages? Do they have to receive forgiveness to get closer to God?
Jacqueline

In all of readings I've done, I haven't heard them "always" saying, "I'm sorry," but when they do, it's not about what they did, but what they didn't do. The life they didn't live. The example they didn't set. The love they didn't show. This is because they know that they see things from a "larger" point of view. They see things differently now that they see the big picture and the effect that their actions had on those they love and on those who love them.

I've heard the souls repeatedly tell their loved ones that the reason why we choose to come here to this plane of existence is to learn a specific lesson that will allow them to experience the Eternal Light of Love more deeply. They also say that when we come here, we forget the lessons we're supposed to learn and for good reason. If we knew what they were, we'd do things because we're supposed to, not because we want to.

When we return and go through our life review, we see the times we remained close to the reason we came here, the lessons we learned, and those we missed.

We also see how our actions and beliefs both benefitted and hurt ourselves and others. We may have been able to justify our selfishness and mistakes in this life, but we can't do it in the next.

If, and when, a soul comes through with an apology during a reading, what it is saying is that it realizes the hurt it caused, and that it is doing the best it can to repair what it did for its own spiritual growth.

Do the souls need our forgiveness to move closer to God?

Do they have to receive forgiveness to get closer to God?
Jacqueline

Your question reminded me of a woman named Marianne who came to one of my seminars. She was hoping to not only learn more about the hereafter, but to also hear from her mother who had passed away. She heard, instead, from her father, and he was the *last* person she had wanted to hear from. Even though her father knew this, he took advantage of the situation and came through during the session, asking Marianne to forgive him. She thought, "Not any time soon, buddy. You hurt me and my mother way too much for me to *ever* forgive you."

The reason why her father came through *knowing* that his daughter didn't want to hear from him is because the souls often know better than we do what we *need* to hear during a session. According to the souls, there's never a point where it's too late to say "I'm sorry," whether it's here or in the hereafter. They also know that there is never a point on our journey that is too late for us to hear how sorry those who hurt us truly are. They do this for themselves, as a necessary part of their own spiritual growth in the hereafter, but they also do it for us—to enable us to put the past firmly behind us where it belongs.

Still, the souls are very aware that while they can communicate their regret, apologize for the unhappiness they caused, tell us they love us, and are working from their world to repair the damage they've done, it's still up to us to forgive. Whether or not we choose to listen and accept their apology is not what they're concerned about—they do it because they will always tell us what we need to hear, whether we want to hear it or not.

Marianne's father knew that she needed to hear what he had to say, even if she wasn't prepared to. Of course, once he said what he had to say, it was her choice to ignore what she had heard because she wasn't ready to forgive and move on.

Marianne told me several weeks later how much it had meant to her to hear that her father understood how much pain he had caused her and her mother. She was now able to find her way back from the pain of her childhood to offer the forgiveness he was asking for. I've heard the same thing from countless numbers of people who have heard the souls of their loved ones asking to be forgiven during their own sessions.

Forgiveness is one of the hardest lessons we have to face while we're here, but it's one that we are here to learn. The souls say that it's only when we can forgive ourselves for what we've done to others, and forgive others for what was done to us, that we can find our way through the hurt and pain in our hearts and move forward in our lives with some peace. By showing mercy towards others, as well as toward ourselves, we learn how to lighten what's been weighing us down. Our soul is able to lift us up just enough to continue moving forward through our journey here, with a better understanding of those who hurt us and a greater acceptance of ourselves as well.

Are the souls of my loved ones paying for my mistakes?

Hi, Anthony,
I am Diana, the lady you read for from Florida back in September. I am the one whose family interrupted your breakfast because they wanted you to be prompt for the reading and they were ready before you.

My mother, father, sister, grandma, and son came through during my session with you, and my friend John who worked with me stopped by to say he loved me. Jerry also stopped by to let me know he is in spirit, and I passed the message on to my husband Antonio (Tony). He is the one that both my son and father approved of after Daddy let it be known I have been married three times. (Thanks, Daddy for the newscast.)

I am very happy that you described my son as a polite young man. That description lifted my heart which has always been so full of love for my Eddie from the day he was born until he left me two days before turning five months. Now my baby boy has grown up into a polite, loving, and especially forgiving man; I am so proud of him. His forgiveness has healed a hole in my heart and my soul that I have been carrying for the last thirty-eight years since he went back home. I felt like an unfit mother because of the events that led to his being born a very sick preemie. I had no idea of the facts until it was too late to correct. I have been kicking my butt all these years for being so freaking naïve.

I know that our loved ones keep tabs on our lives back here in these earthly dimensions. This question is in reference to all the errors and mistakes I have made since my loved ones returned home. There was a time after I lost my son and later my parents that I lost all sense of perception and made some extremely dumb and sometimes dangerous mistakes. I lost my common sense and sought the worst ways to heal my pain and loneness. When I woke up from this fog, I realized that I must have made them very frustrated and at times disappointed because of my actions. In retrospect I feel guilty because my actions may have affected their spiritual growth in Heaven.
Diane

The good news is that nothing you do here can adversely affect the spiritual growth of your loved ones in Heaven. Despite what you may have heard people say, your grief doesn't keep your loved ones from moving on in the hereafter either. Your loved ones are watching you and guiding you from a place of love, hope, peace, and joy as you continue to learn the lessons you're supposed to learn while you're still here.

The souls on the Other Side know that you did what you did so that you could learn the lessons you're here to learn. Life here is difficult, and you'll be here until you learn those lessons. When you do, it'll be your time to go back home. Until then, you'll make mistakes. God and the souls understand this.

What you can do to positively affect their spiritual growth are things like praying for your loved ones, friends, and associates on the Other Side; light candles for them, and forgive them for anything they may have done to hurt you, etc.

Speaking of forgiveness, one of the best things you can do for yourself is to quit wishing the past were different and that you hadn't done whatever it was that you did. I've spent a great deal of time with people who were dying and have been privileged to be there when they transitioned. None of them regretted what they did. What they did regret was what they didn't do.

The souls say that everything happens for a reason and that what's important is not what you've done—it's what you learned from having done it. Did you learn to love yourself and others more after making the mistakes you made? Did you learn because of it to treat yourself and others better? Are you still lovable even after messing things up?

These are the questions that you will be asked by God, and yourself, after you cross over and are going through your own life review wherein you will see the reasons behind everything you did. You will understand that the Eternal Light of Love, and the souls of your loved ones, never lost faith in you or your ability to make something good out of any mess you may have made for yourself or others.

CHAPTER

12

Clair What?

*B*ecause I see my ability as being spiritual in origin and purpose, I typically begin my day in meditation and every session with prayer. I also refuse to assume any other part than that of a messenger, a passive receiver, providing a human voice for the souls. I do not call up or invoke spirits. I don't allow questions to be asked during sessions because it's been my experience that the souls will tell their loved ones *exactly* what they need to hear.

I have different abilities through which I receive messages and information during a session: *clairaudience, clairsentience, sympathetic pain,* and to lesser degrees, *clairalience, clairambience,* and *clairvoyance.*

Clairaudience is the psychic sense through which I hear voices of the souls. During sessions I've done I have even heard singing, cats meowing, dogs barks, and gunshots.

Sympathetic pain and *physical sensations* occur when the soul, through means I don't understand, but definitely feel, lets me know what I'm supposed to say by triggering a sensation in my body that I feel as pain or pressure. If the soul passed from a long-term illness, I'll feel my body slowly weaken. If it had a heart attack, I will feel as though I'm having a heart attack. During one session I felt as though I were run over by a semi-truck. This could mean that the soul was either beaten to death or was actually hit by a semi-truck while it was alive. I've also felt as though I were stabbed or shot during sessions.

Clairalience is an ability that allows me to taste a soul's favorite food or in one session the antifreeze a young woman had drunk in order to end her own life.

With *clairambience*, I've smelled scents such as flowers or cigarette and cigar smoke. I was visiting the home of my friend Debbie's brother and sister-in-law when I smelled smoke. "Was there a fire in this house at one time?" I asked. "No."

The smell was so strong I had to follow it up. What I was eventually able to discern was that Debbie's sister-in-law's mother, brothers, and cousins, who had been visiting for a sleepover, all died in a fire that was later determined to have been deliberately set.

Clairsentience is perhaps the hardest for me to describe or explain, be-cause there aren't any equivalents with any of the five physical senses. It's more along the lines of a feeling or hunch I'm receiving during a session. When I'm receiving a message through this particular sense, I'll say, "This feels like a recent passing to me," or "It feels like there was an argument of some sort that happened between you and him before he passed." I can't explain how this feels or how I know what the feeling means, except to describe what it feels like if I were feeling it. For example, there have been many times I have felt a great deal of affection and love towards this total stranger I'm talking to. "He wants me to tell you that he loves you. Not that he loved you, but that he *loves* you."

With *clairvoyance* I'll "see," in my mind's eye, what I'm supposed to say—

faces, symbols, objects, places, events, letters, and numbers. What makes it tricky is that a symbol may have many different meanings. More often than not, the souls will use a combination of clues—some of which can be surprisingly clear or utterly baffling. A car accident may mean that the soul passed in a car wreck, but it could also mean that the person I'm talking to was in an accident. It could mean the passing was accidental.

Along those lines a "new" car may mean a new car. Or it may mean they're acknowledging car repairs which made a car "like new."

If I see a rope tied in knots, it suggests to me that the soul had a bad temper when he or she was alive. A rose with thorns means that the person was difficult to love.

A birthday cake means I'm supposed to acknowledge the birthday of a child. The color of the cake will let me know the sex of the child. A birthday present will suggest an adult.

If I see the image of the singer Tiny Tim, I know that I'm supposed to "tip toe through the tulips," because what I'm about to talk about may be upsetting to my client.

The souls, aware of my Catholic upbringing, will show me distinctly Catholic symbols whether or not they were Catholic while they were alive. When I see the Sacred Heart of Jesus, it suggests that the person coming through suffered while he was alive. Saint Joseph is my symbol that the person died peacefully, either in his sleep unconscious or in a coma. Saint Anthony suggests that the passing was recent.

One day I was sitting in a coffee shop when an elderly woman at the table next to me struck up a conversation. Eventually she asked what I did for a living. When I told her, I could sense her skepticism, so I decided to do an impromptu reading with her during which her husband came through.

I saw, in my mind, a red rose. Red roses are, for me, a symbol suggesting an anniversary of a wedding, or even a passing, has just passed or is coming up soon and that the soul is using the session as an opportunity to acknowledge it. When I mentioned this, she told me, "It's not our anniversary."

I checked again, and I could see red roses. "I'm not saying your anniversary is today, but was it two weeks ago, or perhaps two weeks from now?"

"No," she said, shaking her head. "I know when my anniversary is, and I have no idea why he would be saying that."

"Well, when is your anniversary?" I asked.

"September 29th."

I looked at the date on my cell phone. "That's today," I told her.

Her eyes became wide and filled with tears. "I forgot all about it!" she said. "I can't believe I forgot it!"

I looked at her, smiled, and said, "Happy Anniversary."

All the time I tell people for whom I do readings that something might come up during the session which may not make sense at the time but will later. That's because the messages I'm passing along typically don't make any sense to me, and they're not supposed to. They're supposed to make sense to the person receiving the messages, and that's all I care about.

I did a telephone session for two sisters in California in which their father and the son of one of the women, who took his own life, came through. Her son, Michael, was fun, full of energy, and kept sharing stories that made the three of us laugh. For example, he talked about "stealing a car." His mother told me, "No, I don't know what you're talking about."

"When I say he stole a car," I told her, "I mean he took a car without permission, possibly even your car."

That's when she understood what I was talking about. When her son was three years old, he "stole" her car keys off of the dresser, climbed into her car, turned it on, put it in gear, and sent the car moving forward to crash into their house! When she heard the crash and saw the car in the house, she also saw her son, who was still in diapers, smiling and saying, "Look at what I did, Mommy! Look at what I did!"

Towards the end of the session I told her, "Michael is showing me blue, lots of blue and blue paint." Both of the women said they had no idea what I was referring to. "Is someone's favorite color blue, or did someone paint the walls blue, because I'm also seeing blue paint," I asked.

"No," they told me.

A few minutes later, after we hung up, I received a picture on my cell phone. It was a blue bong, with blue paint, and a blue bracelet on the bowl.

I imagined the following conversation taking place after we hung up—

"Blue? Does that mean *anything* to you, Deb? No? Me neither. By the way, pass the bong over here will you? You know . . . the blue one . . . with the blue paint and the blue bracelet."

Flick. Bubble. Inhale.

"Hmmm . . . I wonder why Anthony kept seeing blue and blue paint during our reading."

I found out *later* that during the reading the sisters were laughing, crying, *and* doing bong hits the entire time, off of this bong! When I mentioned the color blue and the blue paint, they were looking around, saying to each other, "What is blue in here?" There's a lesson here, I'm just not sure what it is though . . .

The next day Kati was talking to her daughter telling her about the bong and that I asked if someone painted a wall blue. Her daughter told her that after Michael's funeral his father painted the walls of his room bright blue.

CHAPTER

13

Why Do the Souls Communicate with Us?

I've come to understand that, as a medium, it's my job to give the souls a human voice so that they can communicate with their loved ones still here on earth. When I'm doing a session with someone, I remain fully conscious, although I do enter what I can only describe as a "daydream state." Still, I don't go into a trance nor do I speak in any voice other than my own. I've even been known to joke during sessions. No one speaks through me, and I don't consider myself to be a "channel." Souls close to those I'm doing readings for communicate their messages to me, and I pass those messages along. The messages can concern the past, the present, and sometimes the future. They might explain away mysteries and reveal the heart's deepest secrets.

I remember a session with someone who was so skeptical that he agreed to sit with me only after his daughter paid for it and once she had received a session from me. Even though he remarried following the loss of his wife, his grief over her loss was still almost more than he could handle, and it was affecting his new marriage.

"You have to do this, Dad. It'll help you deal with mom's death," she told him.

"I'll do it," he told her, "but I'm not expecting much. When it's done, I'm going to tell you how he does it."

Two things stand out for me from that session. One was how his wife came through not only happy, but teasing him about how he was always losing his sock and blaming his son-in-law. He laughed and admitted that was true.

"Your wife is saying that most people lose their socks in the dryer. Not you. You lose yours in the washer?" Tears came to his eyes as he nodded, "Yes." I couldn't believe what I was seeing and hearing next. His wife was showing me one black sock and one white sock. I knew what I was supposed to say next, but I had to ask just to be sure.

"Did you really wear one black sock and one white sock to work?" I asked, laughing.

"I had to!" he said, loudly. "I didn't have any other socks to wear!"

We both got a good laugh out of that one. What I said next brought him to tears though. "Your wife was cremated, yes?"

He nodded.

"She is saying to me that you didn't keep your promise. You disposed some of her ashes as she asked you to, but you kept some too."

For the first time during the session he began crying openly. "Please tell her I'm sorry. I just couldn't do it. I couldn't get rid of all of her ashes like she wanted me to. I needed to keep some of her with me."

I have to admit that this admission and the love with which he said it made me emotional as well. "She wants you to know that it's okay. She understands why you did what you did."

It took us both a few moments to compose ourselves. "There's no way you could have known that," he said to me. "Not even my daughter knew. No one knew that but me . . . and my wife."

The point of a session is not about you being impressed by my ability. It's not about removing your pain completely either. It's about easing your grief for a while by reassuring you that your loved ones are still with you and watching over you.

Are we not supposed to be calling on the dead?

Well, here I go again thinking too much; if you get a chance, please read Deuteronomy Chapter 18 vs. 10-11-12 . . . kind of sounds like we're not supposed to be calling on the dead!
Barb

When I read your question, I didn't even have to read the particular verses because I knew what you were referring to. Honestly, I've heard these verses used against me on several occasions.

For anyone who isn't familiar with the book, chapter, and verses, here it is from the New International Version (I picked this one because it specifically uses the word "medium")—

[10]Let no one be found among you who sacrifices their son or daughter in the fire, who practices divination or sorcery, interprets omens, engages in witchcraft,[11] or casts spells, or who is a medium or spiritist or who consults the dead. [12]Anyone who does these things is detestable to the Lord; because of these same detestable practices the Lord your God will drive out those nations before you.

On the face of it, I agree, it doesn't look good. LOL

Okay, let's take a look at what is being said here. First of all, these verses were written for a group of people who had fled Egypt. The command here is that they embrace the God of their ancestors, their traditions, rituals and beliefs, and reject the religious practices of the land they left.

If you take out the word "medium" and put in the word originally used, "necromancer," you get a better sense of what is being said. "Necromancy" is the practice of asking the dead what the future holds or how we are to conduct our lives.

In all the years I've done this work, the souls have always resisted questions from their loved ones who ask for advice. God prohibits the souls from answering questions about what we're supposed to do with our lives. The reason is that it would take away from our obligation to learn from our lessons as best we can.

I cannot stress this enough . . . the purpose of a medium session is that you understand that death is not the end of life, love, or relationships. The souls want you to know that you are not alone; you haven't been abandoned. Their desire is that they give you hope which will enable you to get up and out of bed and to put one foot in front of the other while you're grieving.

It's not so you can find out who your soul mate is, what job you should take, or what the lotto numbers are. As I'm always telling people, "Don't believe your grandmother, just because she's dead. Trust your heart."

Should I be worried?

Hi Anthony,
I'm trying so hard to believe and have hope . . . I've been to a few mediums and had no one come through . . . why and do I need to worry?
Judy K

There isn't a good reason why no one would come through during a session for you. My first thought is that there are a lot of people out there who believe that they are mediums, but really aren't.

My second thought was that I've had two people who've come to me who told me that they couldn't be "read." Like you, they'd been to mediums before, and no one came through for them. The last time this happened was just this past June. When I started doing her session, her mother came through. "Why is she coming through?" she asked me. "I don't need to hear from her!" The one before her had a similar response to the soul that came through during her session. In both instances, the souls pulled away. It was as though they were saying, "I wanted to talk to you, but if you don't want to talk to me, it's okay." Both times, there were souls waiting their turn to speak, and they pulled their energy away as well. It wasn't that no one came through for them, but the person that they wanted to hear from didn't come through.

When I'm helping souls reconnect with those they've left behind, I'm passive in the process. In other words, whoever "shouts" the loudest gets my attention. Whoever gets my attention is usually the person whom the sitter needs to hear from the most.

Several years ago a woman came to see me, and again, her mother was the one coming through, "speaking" for about thirty-five minutes.

Then I said to this woman, "I have someone else here. A young male is stepping forward saying, 'Hi, Mom.'" She started crying and said, "Oh thank God! That's my son! He's the one I was hoping to hear from. I was starting to become afraid I wouldn't hear from him!"

Her son explained to her that because he had been with his grand-mother since he passed, he wanted her to go first. "That would be him," his mother told me. "My husband and I brought him up to be respectful." The fact that her mother came through first was even more of a validation that she was hearing from her son. If she hadn't been patient with the process, she might have walked away saying that "no one came through" for her during that session either.

The souls want to communicate with their loved ones here on earth. The root of this desire is love, so there's no point in saying that your loved one(s) don't want to talk to you. You have probably just gone to mediums who really weren't able to do what they claimed they could do.

To sum up here, it's been my experience that no one comes to me unless the soul(s) of someone they love, and who loves them, brings them to me. The idea that you've been to more than one "medium" suggests to me that someone does want to speak to you. So, no, I wouldn't worry. You just need to find someone who is truly able to be a bridge between you and those you love on the Other Side.

What should I ask?

How do I get that right message, the one that makes me absolutely certain that my son is safe on a different plane somewhere, so to speak? That he is still with me in spirit and knows what's going on in my life right now?

What question do I ask?

I don't want a little tidbit of validation that someone could pick up by looking on my F.B. profile. I want to know if my boy hears what I say to him. Does he hear me singing the song I've sung to him since he was a little one? I guess what type of validation I'm looking for is like, "He likes your 'Hunter Thompson' poster on your living room wall." I think something no one else would know would do it . . .

The more time passes, the more I miss him. I want to feel his warmth as I feel so cold.
Theresa

Dear Theresa,

If you've read my book, *Communications from the Other Side*, you know that I didn't start out life "talking to dead people." I didn't want to be a medium. I didn't even know what a "medium" was. To top it off, I was skeptical of psychics in general. If I were to have gone to a medium, I would have wanted to hear things like Social Security numbers, street addresses, and such.

Now that I'm doing this work full time, I understand why the souls don't give out information like that. It might have a "wow factor" to you, but they will give you what you need to hear to let you know that you're hearing from them and that they haven't "abandoned" you.

I was doing a session for a woman during which her husband came through. "He wants me to tell you that he loves the fresh cut flowers you got for your home yesterday. He's telling me that he used to do the same thing for you."

I had to wait a few minutes for her to stop crying. "I did get fresh cut flowers yesterday. I did it because it reminds me of him. He used to do that for me all of the time."

The souls work extremely hard to let you know that they are still alive and still with their loved ones here on earth. I said something to a completely skeptical man who came to see me. I mentioned something to him that you could see shook him. "Your wife is telling me that she wanted to be cremated and her ashes scattered, but you couldn't bring yourself to do it. You kept some of them, so you'd have her near you."

"No one knew about that, only me."

That's the point. His wife did know, and by sharing that "evidence" with him, she was letting him know that she was still with him, still loved him, and cares about him. I couldn't have known about this unless she herself told me this.

During a group session with about eight women, I was bringing through a father for his daughter, Tammy. "Was your father a fisherman?" I asked her. She shook her head, expressing no.

"Did he love to eat fish?" I asked. When she shook her head again, I went around the room. "Was your father a fisherman?" I asked each one of the women there. They all shook their heads indicating no. "I don't understand it," I said, going back to Tammy. "I'm sure this is coming from your father. I'm seeing fish, fishing line, fishing poles, even a fishing boat. It seems to me your father wants me to talk about fish, and I have no idea why!"

After the session was done, Tammy came up to me and said, "I have a confession to make. I'm an atheist. I've been one ever since my father died. I came here to see if you were for real.

When you said that my father was coming through for me, I told him, in my head, 'Dad, if this is really you, get Anthony to say the word fish. So that's when you asked me if he were a fisherman. He wasn't, but he did get you to say the word fish.'"

Anyone can read a New Age book, claim to be a medium, and tell you that your loved one(s) are at peace, and still love(s) you. A real medium will tell you things only you would know. How? They're hearing it from your loved one(s).

With that in mind, *legitimate* mediums aren't out to impress you or convince you of anything. The role of a medium is to be the human voice for the souls on the Other Side. We cannot tell you what we are not told. But what you will hear should leave you with little, or no doubt, that death is not the end of life, love, or relationships.

I'm heartbroken after my reading.

I had a miserable mediumship reading today . . . so very heartbroken and disappointed. [It was] very inaccurate. I left after twenty min. She said things that made no sense like his father's mother was there when he crossed over. She is alive and well [and] other things that she was just making up.

I was hoping for a connection . . . I'm so full of grief I hoped it would help. It did not.
Donna

First of all, I just want to say I'm so sorry about your experience with this particular "medium." I was asked earlier this week about how to find a legitimate psychic medium, so I'll answer that question again here.

"Back in the day," it was much easier to find a reputable medium. It was known as "word of mouth." If someone was legitimate, people talked about him. In my case, 98% of the sessions I did were referred to me. The other 2% were people who found my Web site.

These days it's much harder because so many people are saying that they're mediums and may not be, as you discovered.

My suggestion is that next time you want to see a medium, do it the old fashion way. Find someone based on his/her reputation rather than the fee that is charged or isn't charged.

Make sure that the person knows as little about you beforehand as possible. When you sit down with this medium, please give out as little information as possible. When I do a session, I want to know as little as possible. All I want to know is the sitter's first name. I don't ask for pictures, names, relationships, or anything like that.

Personally, I like the sitters I do readings for to keep their answers to "yes," meaning, "I understand," or "no," meaning, "I don't under-stand," for the most part. I'm not 100% accurate and have never claimed to be. I misunderstand what those here on earth are saying all of the time, let alone those on the Other Side. If I get something wrong, I ask the soul(s) to repeat it.

I want whoever is coming through to prove himself to you, not the other way around. Anyone can read a New Age book and tell you that you're loved ones are okay and are still with you. What you want during a reading is evidence that it really is your loved one(s) commu-nicating with you through the medium. Obviously, you weren't get-ting that and you left. Good for you.

I'm truly sorry that you were hurt even more after your experience than before. Please know that there are people who are legitimately able to connect you with those you love on the Other Side.

CHAPTER
14

The Souls Know What
You Need to Hear

One of the criticisms I've heard made by skeptics is that what I say during readings "could apply to anyone." But if you look at our day-to-day interactions with our loved ones, much of what we do is similar to what people do with one another around the world. People tell one another, "I love you," just as billions of people around the world do every day. Does that mean that they're being insincere when they say it?

In many ways, my communications with those in the hereafter are much like those we have with our loved ones and anyone else in our everyday dealings: some are humdrum and some are deep; some are expected and others surprising. The souls have already looked into our hearts, understand what we need to hear from them and why, and address those issues as best they can. Whether we listen or not, whether we accept what we hear or not, whether we believe or not, doesn't matter to them—they will continue to try to reach us and communicate what we need to hear.

I wish that my ability worked the way some people want it to. I wish it worked the way I want it to. But the souls made it very clear to me early on that I work for them, and the sessions will go the way they need them to go, and what needs to be said during a session is what will be said. They are in charge from nearly the start of the session to its finish. So much so that there have been sessions in which the sitter hears from someone they didn't want to. That doesn't mean that those readings had no value. For some people, even the smallest comforts and reassurances they receive during a reading is enough to help them take steps toward learning to cope with their heartache and a number of other problems.

CHAPTER

15

Praying for the Dead

*J*was in a store one day and I mentioned to my father (this was after he had crossed over and before my mother had joined him) that I was going to buy a candle to light for him.

"I'd rather you pray the Rosary for me," he responded.

I can't tell you how many times people have expressed their surprise when their loved ones asked for prayers during a reading. At the same time, I'm often asked how someone can stay connected, and even more than that, hear from their loved ones on the Other Side. My answer, in a word, is prayer—any form of prayer you're comfortable with.

Long before I ever thought of myself as a medium, or even knew what one was, I lived in an apartment that I shared with a female ghost. Due of my Roman Catholic upbringing, I prayed the Rosary every day. I typically either prayed it at home or in a chapel in the seminary a short distance away from where I lived.

I began to notice that when I prayed at home, my awareness of the woman became stronger and stronger. I could literally feel her standing next to me as I prayed.

Not only that, but when I was praying in the chapel, I would hear men and women praying the Rosary along with me, but behind me. When I would turn around to see who had joined me, there was no one there. To be honest with you, I was so freaked out by all of this that I stopped praying this particular prayer.

These days, as a medium, before beginning a session, I always say a prayer along these lines—"May the Lord bless me and keep me. May he cause his face to shine upon me. May he grant me accuracy and peace during this session." I then invite the soul(s) of the sitter to come forward and start communicating with their loved one(s) through me.

One night I was scheduled to do a group session before about thirty people. I had had a busy and hectic day, and I knew I needed to quiet myself before the event started. Not everyone who was there that night was going to get a reading, but I wanted the messages that did come through to have an impact on everyone there. I went off by myself, sat down, prayed, and quieted myself for a few minutes.

The event that night was incredible. I had a clear connection with the souls that came through, and the people who were there were visibly moved by the messages. I knew that it was because I took a few minutes before hand to become quiet within myself.

The next night, before another event, I went off by myself, prayed, and quieted myself before starting. The results were the same.

By the way, if you're wondering, this is not something I'd usually do before doing a reading or any event. What I would do is something like read a book, drink coffee; one time I was even doing my laundry before, and during, a reading I did for my friend, and author, Josie Varga.

Since the two events I've just talked about, I've resumed my "Centering Prayer" practice, twice a day, every day. Centering prayer is a contemplative practice in which the focus is *listening* to God. It has also helped me to better hear the messages of the souls coming through during a reading.

If it works for me, I know it will work for you as well. I've believed, since the beginning of my career, that a medium is the last resort as far as the souls are concerned. We give them a human voice after re-peated attempts on their part to communicate with you haven't worked.

If you want to hear from a loved one who has crossed over, my suggestion is that you set aside a few minutes to invite him or her to connect with you and then be still and listen. Think about this for a moment. If you take the letters in the word "listen" and re-arrange them, you get a whole new word: "silent."

Take a few minutes to be silent so that your loved ones can be heard by you. As a medium, I can tell you that the "waiting list" of those on the Other Side wanting to re-connect with their loved ones here is *long*. I can also tell you that they'd rather communicate with you directly than through me or any other medium for that matter. Make it a priority to set aside a few minutes every day to be quiet and be open to your loved ones who have returned home before you. I'm sure you'll be stunned by what you hear.

CHAPTER

16

Her "Brother" Was In Heaven Too!

was back East doing a series of private and small group sessions when I was contacted by a woman named Mary. She had just finished reading my book, *Communications from the Other Side*, and told a co-worker that she wished she could get a reading from me and wondered how she could do it. "He's here," Mary's co-worker told her and gave her a way to contact me.

When I met Mary, it was at her home. She had four of her six sisters with her. Anytime I do a family session, it's on the condition that everyone present be there to hear from the same soul. Immediately upon starting the session the girls' mother showed up like gangbusters. I saw the opening scenes of the movie, "The Wizard of Oz," in black and white.

"Your mother is showing me the movie *The Wizard of Oz*," I said. "Does that make any sense to anyone here?" *All* of them immediately started crying and nodding their heads yes.

One of the sisters spoke up to explain. "When we were growing up, *The Wizard of Oz* was our favorite movie, and every year for Halloween each of us would dress up as a character from the movie."

Their mother was coming through loud and clear. I remember wishing that all of the souls that came through during their sessions with me would do so as strongly as this woman was. Then I said, "Your mother wants me to tell you that your brother is with her and that he's doing fine."

They all looked at me puzzled and then looked at one another. Mary finally spoke up, "We don't have a brother."

Without even thinking about it, the message came through so strongly, I asked, "Are you sure?"

"Yes," Mary said. "There're seven of us altogether, but we're all sisters. No brothers."

Then I heard it again, "Tell them that their brother is with me, and we're doing fine." So I repeated it. Mary looked at me and shrugged. Then I heard the message that their *brother* was with their mother. "Did your mother have a miscarriage, or did she terminate a pregnancy?"

"I'm the oldest," Mary explained, "but my mother was pregnant before she had me, and she did miscarry."

"Maybe that's it," I said. "I'll see if I can move past this." Still her mother insisted two more times that I tell her daughters that their brother was with her, so I did. They, in turn, had no idea what I was talking about.

The next day I received a call from Mary. "We know what our mom was talking about when she told you our 'brother' was with her."

"You do?" I asked.

Over the years, people calling or emailing me with a new understanding of a message they received during a reading but didn't understand wasn't unusual. Sometimes it would happen during the session, sometimes a few minutes after, days, weeks, or even months later. But how does someone not know about their "brother?"

"My sister Amy was telling her son about the reading and how Mom kept insisting that our 'brother' was with her and how we didn't know what you or she was talking about," Mary told me.

That's when Amy's son said to her, "Mom, don't you remember? Grandmother was always calling Duke your brother!"

"Who's Duke?" I asked.

"My mother's dog," Mary explained.

"Are you kidding me?" I asked, laughing.

"No. My mother never called Duke a dog. She always called him our 'brother.'"

"I don't understand. What do you mean?" I asked.

"For example," Mary explained, "I used to *hate* coming home late from work or a date because my mother would always yell from her bedroom, 'Oh great! You woke your brother up again! Now he's upset! Take your brother out to McDonald's and buy him a cheeseburger so he'll settle down and go back to sleep!'

"Other times she would say, 'Take your brother for a walk. Your brother's hungry. Put some food in his bowl!'"

I couldn't help but howl with laughter! Yes, the pun was intended!

I love this story because it's one of the best examples I can think of in which a pet is brought up during a reading. Countless numbers of souls have told their loved ones of the comfort and joy they felt seeing their furry animals there to greet them when they transitioned from this life into the hereafter.

People are sometimes surprised to hear that their pets are waiting for them in the hereafter, but according to the souls, not only are they waiting for you when your journey here is finished, they are rewarded for their life here on earth as well! Many animals live their lives boldly and patiently even after being mistreated, injured, and even tortured by those they trust to take care of them.

Animals see without judgment, love unconditionally, and give without any expectation of anything in return. They are a perfect mirror image of the Eternal Light of Love, which is why the souls say that cruelty to animals is considered by them to be a serious offense; worse than even brutality to another human being, because animals are at the mercy of those they love. Suffering at the hands of those here who do not understand or care that they were sent here to teach us love, patience, and understanding, they are victims who are unable to speak out for themselves.

But make no mistake about it . . . in the eyes of the Eternal Light of Love animal souls are just as important as human souls. Treating them well, with kindness and compassion, is seen by those on the Other

Side as an indication that our soul has grown to the point that is aware of, recognizes, and treasures pets for what they are to those of us here on earth . . . ambassadors of the Eternal Light of Love.

CHAPTER

17

Is Mediumship a "Sin"?

I was on the phone doing a reading for Stacy and asked her, "I'm hearing the name Eddie. Do you know who that is?" She told me that she didn't. I was able to establish that her husband was coming through along with his father.

"Was husband a mechanic? He's telling me that he worked on cars, or he worked on *his* car," I told Stacy.

"He worked on his car," she said, "but he wasn't a mechanic."

"Well," I told her, "it's close enough for me. He's saying the name Eddie again."

"My mother-in-law had a friend named Eddie, and he helped my husband work on his car."

"Is Eddie a mechanic?"

"Yes."

"Is he still here . . . still alive?"

"Yes"

"You said he's a friend of your mother . . . where's your mother? Is she there?"

"She's in the next room," Stacy told me.

"Go get her. Your husband wants her to be a part of this." I often warn people that the souls will use the opportunity to talk to their loves ones who are still here, especially if they're in the vicinity. Stacy asked her mother-in-law to come into the room after which Stacy's husband and father-in-law both passed along messages. When the session was over, both women were happy. At least, that's what I thought as I hung up the phone.

A week later, I received the following message:

Hi, Anthony, You did a reading for my daughter-in-law Stacy, and my son pulled me into the reading; my father was also there. I am a woman of God; I have been told by everyone I know who is with our Lord that this is evil— the one sin that the Lord will not forgive along the lines of witchcraft, spirit boards, and séances. Please respond to this. I was told since I didn't do the reading, to just ask God to forgive me and tell him I would never do this again. From Deborah

This was hardly the first time I've heard this sort of thing. In fact, the first time was after I had done a reading for a young woman named Marie many years before, when I first started doing readings on the Internet. Her grandmother came through telling her that "Heaven is real. Heaven exists." Marie validated this message for me by telling me that her grandmother was in a coma in the final moments of her life and that everyone in her family spent twenty minutes alone with her. Afraid that she would never see her grandmother again, Marie told her that she needed her to tell her that Heaven is real and that Heaven does exist.

After the reading she called her father and told him about it, thinking her father would be excited to know that Marie had heard from his mother. Rather than being happy, he was outraged. "What he is doing is the work of the Devil," he screamed at her over the phone. He also told her that if she didn't go to church that Sunday and repent, she wasn't invited to the family reunion the next weekend, because she was no longer welcomed in the family. You can imagine how she felt about the reading and about me after that. When she had finished the conversation with her father, she got on the phone and screamed at *me*.

I was doing these Internet readings to try to figure out if I really was hearing from those who had passed away. By the time I had done Marie's reading, I was pretty much convinced I was connecting with the dead, not that I was crazy about the idea. After hanging up with her, I thought to myself, "That's it. I'm done. I'm going back to my life the way it used to be."

The next thing I heard in my head was, "It's my desire that you to do this for the rest of your life." What I heard was so gentle and so loving that I had no doubt that the voice I heard was from God.

I was sitting in a Starbucks connected to a Barnes and Noble "superstore" at the time. I immediately got up and went to the back of the store. I looked around to make sure no one was near, and I began to pray at the top of my lungs, "Are you CRAZY? You cannot ask this of me! I thought you were supposed to be omniscient! This is the stupidest thing I've ever heard!" To say that I was upset was an understatement.

I didn't understand why I was being asked to continue doing the work or even what purpose it served. I wasn't sure it served any purpose at all. No one I had done readings for before that got back to me to tell me it had made any sort of impact on their lives. Marie was the first and that was to tell me her father thought I was an agent of the Devil, if not Satan himself!

For the next several weeks I went to daily Mass at the Catholic Church near me, wondering if I were, in fact, offending God. After Mass was over, I would remain behind, crying and praying, "Am I doing something wrong here? Am I offending you?" The answer to my prayers was always, "It is my desire that you do this for the rest of your life."

Someone told me that he was sure that I'm doing what God wants me to do. "I sure hope so," I told him. "Otherwise, I've been wasting both of our time."

Is what you're doing the work of the Devil?

Hi, Anthony,
I was raised super religious and taught that psychics, horoscopes, anything

*like that was the Devil's work and to avoid at all costs. Not to offend, but
you know that's what most teach. What is your thought on that?
I know you and have known you for a very long time so I know that is not
true of you, but how does someone with that belief and background reconcile himself with your work? Just wondering your thoughts?
Carmen*

Thanks so much for asking this question! I originally wrote a really
long answer, then I remembered what the souls are constantly trying
to tell me—I don't have to prove anything or change anyone's mind.
My job is to simply share what I've learned from doing this work. That
being said, I'll answer your question primarily from the work I do.

I've been accused of being in league with the Devil more times than
I can remember. Usually, I'll say, "If that's the case, Satan picked the
wrong guy to do this work, because I've been delivering the messages
all wrong."

I've also been told that the souls who come through during sessions are really demons masquerading as loved ones of the people
who come to me for readings. If that's what's going on, they're even
bigger boobs than I am as far as doing this work goes.

Several years ago I did a reading for a young woman whose boyfriend was murdered when he tried to leave the gang he was in. When
he came through, after providing enough details about his life to assure her it was really he, he told her he was at peace with what happened and had forgiven those who had murdered him. He also kept
insisting that he wanted her to not only forgive his killers, but to also
pray for them!

Even I was amazed at the peace and joy this young man was radi-
ating. The only thing that seemed to be troubling him was the idea
that someone might try to avenge his death!

"He wants you to call, literally call on the phone, *anyone* who has
said he's going to get revenge for his murder. He doesn't want anyone
else to die because of this. He wants you to promise him that you'll do
this."

That's hardly the attitude I would have expected from a "demon"
pretending to be someone it's not.

People have come to me for readings who have lost all faith in God and tell me later that their faith has been restored after hearing from their loved ones. People who thought that life wasn't worth living found the strength to keep putting one foot in front of another after hearing that their husband, wife, son, or daughter isn't lost to them, but walking beside them. I've seen relationships repaired, after parents on the Other Side ask their children to forgive them for what they did, while they were here in this life.

Love is a much greater force than all the acts of evil ever done. Love is the reason the souls want to communicate with those they have left behind. Love is the reason God wills, and allows, communication between the souls and their loved ones to happen.

I believe that most of the people, who say what I do is the work of the Devil, are sincere in what they believe, but are misinformed and afraid. I just wish that they would put their fears aside, get a reading themselves, and see if they still feel the same way afterwards.

Every time I do a reading and I see hope rising out of the ashes of despair, I know God is the source, not some "devil," and it's how I reconcile what I do with the anger and ridicule that are occasionally directed towards me for doing it.

How do we know for sure it's "good souls"?

What if it's indeed bad and it's playing tricks on us? Sorry for a silly question but often wonder.
Kristy

I'll admit that when I started doing the work, I often wondered the same thing. I've done this work for a several years now, and in the countless numbers of sessions I've held, I've never heard anything close to being malicious said by a soul to its loved ones here. I will say, though, that I've heard from other people who have been to so-called mediums that they have. Whenever I hear this, though, I think it's a result of their (the medium's) own personal beliefs, or misunderstandings, and not anything they've heard from the souls on the Other Side.

I'm not a "New Ager." I didn't attend development circles. Many of the beliefs I had when I started doing this I've since let go of . . . sometimes grudgingly so. My training has been "on the job" after being thrust into it by the Eternal Light of Love and the souls. I didn't choose to do this work; it chose me. I'm still learning, and what the souls are teaching me by communicating with their loved ones still here I'm passing on to whoever is willing to listen. What they talk about is the unconditional love of God, forgiveness, and hope. They share that one day we'll all be together again in a place in which love is the standard and the rule by which all who are there live. Hardly what I would think I'd be hearing about if they were "dark" or "evil."

Whenever I do a reading, I invite only souls that are "in the light of God" to come through during a reading. In other words, I'm bringing through only souls in the higher levels of enlightenment, who are closer to the Eternal Light of Love.

Plus, I don't think that the souls in lower levels have any interest in speaking to me to begin with. They're too "immature" spiritually to want to reach out to those who are still here.

The other way that I know that they are "good souls" is because of the messages that do come through. They're meant to reassure and comfort their loved ones still here and to let them know that death is an illusion. They are happy, very much alive, and in a place of peace and bliss with the Eternal Light of Love. They speak of the joy that awaits us when it's our time to return home and be reunited with them.

Again, that hardly sounds, to me at least, like someone "evil" who is trying to deceive us. I think that "evil" ones would be trying to make us unhappy or depressed. As I said before, I have heard of people who have walked away from readings unhappy and depressed, but that's because of, in my opinion, the deluded beliefs of the "medium" and not anything the souls would honestly say to their loved ones.

How do I know that it's not my own beliefs that are deluded? Because I used to think some of the same things I've heard said. Thankfully, the souls gently and patiently would not allow me to say things that weren't correct during readings I was doing, literally. I would open my mouth to interject something that I believed, and that might have unwittingly hurt the person I was talking to, and nothing would come out.

Finally, I've been told that there aren't any "bad" souls on the Other Side. Are there souls who have committed evil acts while they were here? Absolutely, there are. But after going through their life review, they see not only what they did, why they did it, the havoc their acts created, how they affected others, but also what they need to do to repair the damage, if that's what they choose to do.

Have you ever contacted a soul from hell?

Have you ever contacted a soul that went to hell!??? Just curious . . . no one ever admits it if so . . .
Shana

I'll be the first to admit that when I began doing this work, I believed in the existence of "hell," where demons and devils existed and from where they would make our lives miserable. After all, "misery loves company." So I made sure to take every precaution so that I would *not* hear from "dark entities." Still, for a time, I wondered if I were being duped by "demons" that were using me to tell people things that weren't true.

When the movie *Ghost* with Patrick Swayze, Demi Moore, and Whoopi Goldberg came out, my favorite scenes were when the two murderers were dragged away by "dark entities" into "hell." As I was watching this, silently cheering this "eternal justice," the souls told me that what I was seeing wasn't the way it worked. I told them I didn't want to hear it.

During readings, the souls would insist that "hell" doesn't exist. It caused me a great deal of sleepless nights.

"What if I were being duped by 'demons' or 'dark entities' and unwittingly deceiving those coming to see me for a reading?" I'd wonder. After all, some of the things I heard the souls admitting to having done while they were here on earth, being human, I would think, "If *anyone* deserves to go to hell . . . "

I was doing a group session one night when I said to one of the women there, (I'll call her Brenda), "Do you know the name Brian, living or deceased?" She nodded her head. "He wants you to know that he loves you, and while his journey on the Other Side is a long one, he's doing the best he can to make up for the hurt he caused. Do you understand this?" She nodded her head again. "He keeps insisting that I tell you he's with God and at peace."

I heard from her again the next day. "I told my daughter about the reading you gave me last night. She kept calling me back and asking questions. She kept asking me if her brother was okay. I told her you said he was, but she kept calling me until four o'clock this morning! Do you think that you could fit my daughter and me in for a private session before you leave town?"

I told her I would be happy to. We met a couple of days later. This time her daughter was with her.

After the session began, Brian came through again, thanking his sister for taking care of his young son after his passing. A short time later, a woman came through claiming to be Brian's wife. She brought two little girls with her. All of them assured Brenda and her daughter that they were fine. Then I saw a vision that made me so emotional they had to wait for me to compose myself before continuing.

A week before I was on a "cemetery ghost tour" with a few friends. I had become so bored that I broke away from the group and went off on my own.

I found myself in front of four-person headstone: a man, a woman, and two children between them. I became aware of another stone with the name of a young woman to my left. There were pictures of two young boys in front of it. I don't know how, but I *knew* that the young woman buried there was somehow connected to the plots I was standing in front of.

My friends caught up with me and asked me what I was looking at. I told them. After a few minutes they suggested we continue with the "tour." As I was leaving, I said a silent prayer, "If you want to connect with anyone in your family who is still here, feel free to bring them to me. The following Thursday I met Brenda during the group session.

I realized that I had been standing in front of the graves of the four souls who had been in front of me just a week before. That's when Brian told me that he had killed his estranged wife and his two daugh-ters when she came to pick them up from his home to take them all to a local children's restaurant. He shot his son as well, but he survived. Brian then turned the gun on himself.

Even though, as a medium, I'm told by the souls not to get in-volved, I'm still human. I became angry at what I heard, and especially that Brian was at "peace" with what he had done.

"If anyone deserves to go to hell," I thought, "it's this guy."

The truth is though, he wasn't in hell. According to the souls, hell doesn't exist.

Did you know that the word "hell" actually has its origins in real estate? There was nothing ungodly or negative about the word. "Hell" is a word from old English which meant "fence" or "pen." If you wanted to keep a cow or pig confined you would "hell" the animal by building an enclosure for it. Then the creature is "helled," which is where the word "held" comes from.

Hearing the souls being so blasé when they talked about what was done to them, stressing that their loved ones hear their message about the need to forgive . . .

Slowly, it dawned on me that if I am hearing from "demons," their messages of love and comfort meant that they're failing "the Devil" miserably. I realized that all of the medium sessions I've ever done, and I've done the work for several years now, were motivated by love. The souls ask to allow this communication with their loved ones to happen, and God grants permission, out of love for those of us trying to find the strength and courage to carry on. People have come away from their sessions with me comforted and happy. People who were angry with God found their faith again.

What "evil" purpose does that serve?

Having said that, I will admit that I have done readings in which the person who came through wasn't someone I would have spent time with in this plane of existence, but they didn't come to be friends with me to begin with.

Secondly, they make themselves known the way they were known here. That doesn't mean that's the way they are in the hereafter however. It's just that the closer they come here to earth during a reading, the more they take on the same personality while they were here.

I did a reading for a young woman (nineteen years old) whose father literally drank himself to death. Her mother and father separated, and later divorced, when she was twelve years old. He admitted to not being a very nice guy and not a very good father at times, being abusive to her, her mother, and brother.

What struck me throughout the reading was how much she still loved and adored him and how happy she was to find out he was still in her life. If she can forgive him and love him as much as she does to the point that she is happy to hear that he's found the peace that eluded him here on earth, how can we expect any less from the One the souls call Eternal Light of Love?

CHAPTER

18

Dark Angels

I did a reading over the phone for a wonderful woman named Ginny, who lives in Tucson, AZ. Early on she wondered if she could ask questions, something I normally don't allow during a session. The reason for this is that it's been my experience that the souls know what you need to hear. They will often answer questions before they're even asked.

The other reason is that when someone is preoccupied with a question, such as, "I want to know if my mom can tell me when I'm going to meet my soul mate?" they probably aren't listening to the information and evidence being given by the souls of their loved ones.

After Ginny's husband, Ed, pulled his energy away, Ginny wanted to validate for me some of the messages that came through. We talked about Ed saying that he was aware that she was holding his hand until the hospice staff literally took him away. She asked me if it were possible that his spirit left long before his body stopped breathing.

"Absolutely," I told her. I've heard from many souls who told their loved ones that their spirit left their body before the actual moment of "death."

Ginny told me that she was wondering about this because as she sat by her husband's side, holding his hand, waiting for him to cross over, she heard and saw angels singing songs that were "surreal and ethereal." The thing that scared her was that the "angels" were "dark."

"They might not have been angels," I told her. She disagreed, telling me again how she heard them singing.

"I hear what you're saying," I told her. "I'd like you to hear what I'm saying." I went on to explain that when her husband passed away, she thought of it as "there he goes," and it's a moment of sadness. For God, and those on the Other Side, it's "here he comes," and it's a reunion they rejoiced over. That would explain the singing.

I also explained to her that when souls appear to me, they are often "dark." The reason for this is not because they are "evil," although I'm sure some would argue otherwise, claiming I'm being duped by the "Devil." It's because they're standing with the light of God behind them. The reason for this is that God is the one who wills this to take place, and all the communication that happens is done in the presence of God.

The first time I saw the cover of my book, *Communications from the Other Side*, I emailed Jennie Taylor Martin, the marketing director of 4th Dimension Press to tell her how excited I was because that's what I "see" during readings. As far as I was concerned, the person who designed the cover did so inspired by the souls themselves.

When all was said and done, Ginny was relieved that what she saw and heard weren't "demons" singing at the imminent demise of her husband. This also explained to me why she continually needed to be reassured that her husband was "okay" during our time together.

I cannot stress this enough as far as the souls are concerned. *No one* is ever lost to God, and if they're not lost to God, they're not lost to you.

Do evil people live in Heaven?

Do evil people REALLY end up in the paradise that the other souls pres-

ently live in? Evil people like animal abusers, sexual deviants, pedophile clergy, etc.

Each time I read about another animal being neglected or abused to near death, my heart hurts; I feel so helpless.

How does one bring Light and Love to such dark and evil people? It's difficult for me to comprehend that God made such evil beings, though I do KNOW that's a learned behavior.

Andrea

I was talking to someone on the phone and we had a similar conversation. I told her, "Let's pretend that God appoints you judge for a few minutes. What sins do you condone and what do you condemn?"

As we talked she realized that she would condone the "sins" she commits and condemns those she doesn't. I'm sure that would be true of each one of us.

What if God decided to appoint someone like Al Capone as judge? Think about it. This is the same guy who said, "I don't know why everyone is coming after me. I didn't do anything to hurt anyone."

God does appoint every one of us as "judge" of ourselves during our life review. Personally, I'd rather God judged me, since I've been told by the souls that God doesn't make mistakes but understands when we do.

So the answer is "yes." Souls that have done evil while they were here are in "Paradise," and they're grateful they are there. But the souls have explained to me what's it's like for them. They described it in terms of seasons. The closer that the earth's tilt brings us to the sun, the more we feel the warmth of the sun. The farther away, the less we feel its warmth.

For souls that have wreaked havoc during their time here, at the end of their life review they place themselves on a "level" farther away from God. However, having experienced God's love, their want is to repair the damage they caused and lessen the degree of separation they feel from God.

The souls have repeatedly told me that there is no hell except for the hell we create here on earth and that evil exists here on earth. This is the reason why our common purpose is to recreate heaven here on earth. We do this by being a reflection of the Eternal Light of Love to

one another. By raising your consciousness you raise the consciousness of those around you. In my opinion, people are fixated on the
wrong things, like evil. They should be worrying about how they can
make the world a better place by being models of hope, love, caring,
understanding, compassion, generosity, and peace in a world that has
outwardly gone mad.

Your "job," as well as mine, is to bring light to wherever we find
darkness. We do this by loving those who are hurting so much that
they feel justified in hurting others— hate the "sin," not the "sinner."

It's here on earth that we experience violence, pain, poverty, fear,
and hate. In the world where the souls live, there is only peace, love,
and joy. There have been many times during a reading that I'll hear a
soul talk about the cruel things it did to its loved ones and others
while it was alive. I'll think, "Where's the justice?" but the souls have
made it clear to me, many times, that while someone may get away
with breaking man's law, no one gets away with breaking God's law.
While the lower levels these souls put themselves in may be heaven,
it's not a walk in the park by any stretch of the imagination.

How do the Eternal Light of Love and the souls see us?

*Are we perfect on the Other Side in Eternal Love and how does each soul
see us?*
Jacqueline

I received my certification in Spiritual Direction (Spiritual Coaching)
back in 1999. When I had hung up my shingle and was nervously waiting for my first client to arrive, I heard a familiar voice in my head say,
"I want you to see this person the same way I see all of my children."

"How do you see us?" I asked.

"Perfect."

We are perfect on the Other Side, and we are perfect here. How is
that possible? Because we are not humans with a soul, we are souls
that have taken on the role of being human to learn lessons in love.

One question I've asked the souls is, "If we're 'perfect' in the eyes of
God, then why do we come here?" The answer they keep giving me is,
"To recreate heaven on earth and to reflect the Eternal Light of Love to

one another. We do this by facing the trials and tribulations of life on earth and by doing our best to love ourselves and one another while we're going through them. By doing this we earn the right to experience more deeply the Eternal Light of Love when we return home."

The souls see us the same way that the Eternal Light of Love sees us, with exception that they would say that we're "capable." In other words, they see us with the hindsight that comes from having lived life in this "vale of tears." They know that what they went through was not only necessary for their spiritual growth, but what happens to us is also necessary for ours as well. They know that whatever the challenges are that we face, we can not only handle them, but that we will also learn from them in the end.

That's why they cannot interfere with our lives here. They can guide us along our journey, but they wouldn't think of taking anything away from us—no matter how painful. They can only watch and counsel us that in the end we'll give thanks for all of it. They also tell us that no matter how hard things are, you can get through them, and when you do, you'll be better off for it.

Being Roman Catholic, a soul that the Church recognizes as a saint told me, when I was complaining about what was happening in my life, "We cannot interfere in what is happening in your life, not even God can. It would take away from the lessons you're here to learn. But we can reassure you that in the end there's Heaven!'

How do the souls see us?

Speaking of our loved ones being able to see us . . . I read something today that kind of confused me. Another author claimed our loved ones don't "see" us in our human form but in a haze or as auras of light. As I said, confusing.
Jan

Jan, since I don't know to what book you're referring, I don't know why the author is saying that. I can say that when I started investigating hauntings and such, I visited an apartment building which the tenants were saying was active. The building had storage and a laundry room in the basement that I was told was so active the tenants refused to do their laundry there.

I went down into the basement with a couple of my team members at the time, and I stepped into a "vortex." I can't put into words what it felt like, but I will tell you that when I looked at the two people with me they did seem to be hazy. In fact, the entire room seemed like I was looking through glass smeared with a Vaseline film. That *may* be what this author is referring to, but I believe I saw things the way those who haven't crossed over see us.

When I'm doing a session, the souls talk about seeing their loved ones *very clearly*. They also say that they are closer to us in a way that was *impossible* when they were still here. They will often bring up things that happened that seem superficial to let their loved ones know that they're still around. One young man talked about his mother cooking lasagna the night before her session with me and how she told him, "I'm going to talk to Anthony tomorrow, and you'd better show up."

During a seminar I told a woman that her husband was showing me a full moon in the sky. I asked her if he ever told her he loved her to the moon and back. "No," she said.

"Why would he keep showing the full moon?" I wondered out loud. She shrugged her shoulders.

After the seminar we were talking and I mentioned the full moon her husband kept showing me, psychically. "The only thing I can think of is that I was standing on my deck last night, looking at the full moon and thinking of him."

"Oh, is that all?" I asked her, shaking my head.

Do we have any privacy from the souls?

I've often wondered just how much of our thoughts are available to our loved ones. Is there is a line that they cross between private thoughts and public thoughts per se? Do they know our every thought good and bad, even if it's about someone else? I have just been kind of curious about this.
Stacy

Are the souls monitoring your every thought, word, and deed from the Other Side? In a word, "No." The good news is that the souls are way too busy on the Other Side to be "busy bodies," when it comes to our thoughts.

The even better news is that when we do need them, they are only a thought away. All you have to do is think of them, and they are right there with you. When you pray for them, they are with you. When you need their prayers, they are with you.

When souls go through their life review, they see the reason for everything that happened in their lives, the lessons they contained, and who they became as a result of having gone through all of it. It is all seen as a necessary part of their journey, including their thoughts when they were going through it. That being the case, while they are accompanying you on your journey, they are aware that it's your journey, and everything that happens is also a necessary part of it. They know, from personal experience, that your thoughts are also part of your journey as well, and not something "good" or "bad." They don't judge your thoughts nor do they care what you're thinking. It's more along the lines of, "This is happening because this is what they're thinking." Because of that they might try to inspire you to see things differently so that you'll feel differently or get a different result.

The souls have said that their primary concern on the Other Side is that you stay as close to your purpose while you're still here as possible—learning lessons about love so that you'll reap the greatest rewards when you return back to them. They are watching you, guiding you, and trying to help you, not out of judgment or because they now know better than you, but because they've been where we are now. They see everything with the 20/20 vision that comes with hindsight, and they want you to know what they've learned—that everything that is happening in your life is an opportunity to learn to love yourself and others because of it.

What they are *not* doing is watching you take a shower and thinking to themselves, "You know, you really could stand to lose twenty pounds! Just saying . . . "

CHAPTER

19

You Need to Hear This!

Once souls experience their life review, it seems as though part of their journey in the hereafter is to share with their loved ones here what they've learned. They want to let their loved ones know that they're very much alive and still with us.

Every once in a while someone will say to me, "I wish I had your ability." When I hear this, I'll say, "I do too. I could use the break." The souls have told me that they chose me to do this work because I came here to teach people hope. The souls would tell you that you don't have to be a medium to hear from them.

I've heard many incredible stories from people on this side of the veil who have experienced and even seen their loved ones who have crossed over, both in dreams and in waking moments. Others have told me about feeling connected to their loved ones in other ways, such as with smells, seeing butterflies and heart-shaped clouds as well as hearing a song at the exact time they were thinking of their loved one.

The issue we have is that we tend to dismiss these experiences as wishful thinking. Scientists even have a term for it: "grief psychosis." Is that to say that because you're grieving the loss of someone you love you are susceptible to delusional thinking? The truth is what's really going on in many cases is that the souls care enough about you to make their presence known to you, even if it's just for a moment, to let you know that they're still with you in order to restore your hope.

Our loved ones try in a number of ways to let us know that they're near—so many ways that describing them would fill a book. But some of the most common ways are dream visitations, smells, and manipulating anything electrical.

Of course, I can't talk about this without talking to those who don't think that they've received any signs at all. I've heard from many people who have told me that they think it means that their loved ones no longer recognize them, which is never the case. The souls have told me that when we're ready to receive and understand a sign from them, we'll receive it. Sometimes the signs they send are so subtle that their loved ones miss them completely, because they're expecting a "burning bush."

The souls of your loved ones want you to know that they are with you; you are never alone, especially during those times when you're feeling most alone or frightened. Part of their journey and growth is to guide you on yours while you're here, and it's something they do out of love for you. They are happy and more than willing to do this as often as it takes until you are reunited with them on the Other Side.

Is this song a sign?

While I have never been a huge fan of Anne Murray, the artist, my mother, who has just earned her wings, was. The song "Broken Hearted Me" keeps coming on the radio; as I have never been a fan, I don't know the song, but I found myself drawn to it, listening to the words very intently. But by the time I realize it's on, it's over.

The medium reading I had with you was absolutely amazing. Mom came through saying I was right about several things: she should have turned up her oxygen, she had diabetes, she was married to a gangster (my father), and of course that she is okay. At the end, you told me that she said she had to go, Jesus was calling her . . . it was that part of the reading that had made me realize she was going on . . . going on without me.

Now, I know it's selfish, but I couldn't help but feel like I was saying goodbye AGAIN; something I had never ever felt ok with, so to speak. Yet I knew that you were in direct contact with her, and she was okay with it. Listen, my mother and I were always a team, so this wasn't something I would have expected—our separation and her being okay with it. I would be lying if I said that didn't bother me.

Anyway, back to this song that keeps playing that I have never heard, but by an artist that I know she adored. Finally tonight I looked up the song and lyrics, the part that has me thinking this song is a visit from Heaven, goes " . . . when you hear this song, I hope that you will see that time won't heal a broken-hearted me." Is this in my head or a legit visit from my mother? Could I have mistaken her message crossing over to the spirit world wrong? Is it possible that she is just as broken-hearted as I am and this is her way of letting me know???

Something is telling me yes, and that she is where she belongs now. I am to go on with all her love encapsulated within until we meet again, to appreciate the time we had, and to build on the strengths she left me, not the weakness that she NEVER condoned, even in the end.

What do you think?
Lisa

I try to make it clear to people who receive readings from me that a session with me, or any medium, cannot take away your grief, and they're not meant to. A reading helps you understand that "death is not the end of life, love, or relationships," that your loved one hasn't left you, and that you are never alone.

Having said that, I'm sure you've heard the saying, "You can't take it with you when you die." Well, love is the *only* thing that the souls bring with them to the hereafter. Love is even more powerful than death, and all the love you shared with her is returned back to you from the Other Side.

Now that she is where she is, she can see straight into your heart, and all the love that you have for her. Not only that, but she's able to be with you in the dark moments you miss her most, feeling all alone.

Because of that, she doesn't feel the same pain of separation you do.

The reason you may be hearing this song so often, and why it may be a visit or a sign from your mother, is that she also understands that a part of your journey and lessons during this time is to endure the pain of her passing. She *cannot* take away the pain you're feeling because you're supposed to learn during this time to love again and to find hope and peace while you're suffering her loss. What she can do is help you find a reason to keep going while you're still here.

That could be the meaning behind the words, " . . . when you hear this song, I hope that you will see that time won't heal a broken-hearted me." She's letting you know that grief will be a part of who you are until you're reunited with your mother again on the Other Side.

To her, it will seem like a blink of an eye until she sees you again. For you, it's day after day of putting one foot in front of the other until the time you earn the same love, joy, and peace that she is experiencing in her new home.

It might help you to think of her love for you as a beacon of light leading you back to her when your work here is done. In the meantime, until that glorious day comes, please know that she continues to walk with you, sharing in your joy and pain, helping you help yourself until you see her again. You are not alone, you are still a team, and you'll never be without her, no matter how much it feels as though you are.

Do our loved ones "rest in peace"?

Do we really want them to REST? I know I don't want my loved ones to rest as I want them to talk to me and tell me things. I am waiting for the day that I can get validating messages from them; at least that is how I feel at this moment!!
Sherry

According to the souls, the last thing they are doing is "resting" on the Other Side! As soon as they cross and have gone through their life review, they know they have "work" to do. One thing the souls have repeatedly said is that part of their journey is to help us stay on track with ours. Now that they've seen the answer sheet to all of life's questions, they want to help us so that we'll learn what they now know, before it's our time to leave this life.

In other words, Sherry, your loved ones are talking to you and telling you things! Every day that you wake up, stay true to your purpose, learn a new lesson from the struggle as you move through your grief. *You* validate the messages you are receiving from them.

The souls are not "resting" but living in community, doing work that they love, that brings them joy, and what they need to do to progress on their own spiritual journey. They are watching over you, inspiring you to stay on yours.

You mentioned that you want "validating messages." I meet people all of the time who receive signs to the point it hurts them more than it helps. In my first book I wrote about one woman who asked me during a session why she wasn't receiving any more "signs" from her three children who had passed away. They told her it was because she had become dependent on them and that she needed to move on with her life. Of course, that was the last thing she wanted to hear, but when she realized that they were right, she started working with other bereaved mothers. The next time she came to me for a session, her children told her that they couldn't be more pleased.

The souls of our loved ones know what we want. More importantly, they know what we need. Our task is to trust that they know what they're doing and that we'll receive signs from our loved ones when we need them the most.

If, however, they are trying to communicate with you and for whatever reason you're unable to receive or understand the messages they're sending, then they'll send you to someone like me—someone who is able to act as a bridge between the here and the hereafter and to give them a "human" voice.

Why haven't I received a sign?

Everyone that I have been reading gets signs. Bobby has been gone since 10/4/13, and I have nothing. He is just gone. I feel stuck and cannot move forward. I feel like I'm waiting for him. I've been making bargains and of course, nothing.

How can I get him to give me a sign?
I talk to him constantly. I'm going crazy. Please respond.
Debra

I can certainly understand how frustrated you must feel when it seems as though everyone else but you is receiving signs from their loved ones in the hereafter. It makes you wonder if your loved one is okay and still loves you. I can assure you that the answer to both questions is, "Yes."

The souls are able to communicate with you from the moment they pass over, and they do so for a number of reasons. One of them is to destroy the myth that everything ends with death. They also want to give you hope and encouragement to keep putting one foot in front of the other on your journey through grief so that you'll persevere until the day comes when you'll be reunited in a world of bliss and peace.

So why is it that some people don't seem to receive signs?

First of all, I want to say right off the bat that the souls of your loved ones know you want and need to hear from them. They also want you to know that they are happy and that you will be reunited when it's your time to go back home. They also know when is the right time to send you a sign and in a way that is best for you.

I have a friend named Debbie who lost her best friend in a hit-and-run "accident" several years ago. When we met, she knew what I do but never said a word about Eric. I had known her for a couple of months, and when I was visiting her, he came through for her while we were watching television. Afterwards, Debbie told me that she was so depressed that she seriously considered taking her own life at one point.

The next day, while I was taking a shower, Eric showed up again to thank me for being the bridge which allowed him to communicate with Debbie. "Why did you wait so long to talk to her?" I asked him.

"She wasn't ready," he answered.

When I tell people this story, I often hear, "But I am ready." My impression is that what they're saying is that they're ready for a sign in a way that they want to receive it.

The truth is that the souls have never stopped talking to us here on earth, and you don't need a "medium," or to be one, to hear them. Their communications come in many forms and not necessarily in the way you may want them to, but in a way that they know is best for you. Signs may appear in the form of words that come to us in dreams or visitations. Or they may seem like random events or coincidences that we easily dismiss but are meant to let you know that your loved one is still with you or to bring your attention to something specific you need to think about. They may also come to you in the form of a person who shows up in your life—someone who can make a real difference in the way you live or think.

You're not alone, no matter how much it may feel that way. They know exactly what will help keep you on your path, learning the lessons you're here to learn, keeping the fire of hope burning within you. The souls work hard to create opportunities and circumstances to make the journey through grief a little easier for their love ones to travel.

For that reason they send us carefully chosen signs which may not be as obvious as seeing a cloud in the sky or a heart-shaped stone, or coins with dates that match their birthdates, etc. It may just be through someone who writes a book answering questions from those who are grieving.

CHAPTER

20

The Reason is Love

*L*ove is the reason why we choose to come here. For many people connecting with others in love relationships is a part of their soul's intention while they're here on the earth. People meet, fall in love, and continue their journey together. There's a lot of truth behind the idea of matches "made in Heaven," because that's often what has happened. Two souls plan on meeting here on earth to help each other's spiritual growth. Since they come here with any memory of their lives on the Other Side and their spiritual goals wiped away while they're here, it seems to them and to everyone else that their meeting one another was purely by chance. Ultimately, the "how" of people meeting here is less important to the souls than the "why" they met, which is to share a beautiful journey that empowers them to grow spiritually.

What's most interesting, to me at least, is that in the sessions I've conducted, I've heard stories from the souls of lives lived in every possible way imaginable. I've heard the good, the bad, the ugly, and the awe-inspiring. But the one common idea I hear is that the one thing we take with us from this life into the next is the love we've given and the love we received. All of the other emotions that can overpower us in ways greater than love—hate, anger, hurt, jealousy, fear, hopelessness, depression—no longer exist within us when we return to the hereafter.

Do the souls remember experiencing these emotions? Absolutely they do, but in a way that is only a distant memory to them. It is so distant that when they do talk about it, it's one of those, "Oh yeah, that . . . " sort of memories, especially for those who've been home for longer periods of time.

Get them talking about the subject of love, though, and the entire conversation is transformed. They speak of the love they received in terms of the here and now. When the souls speak of their lives here, it's not wealth, power, and prestige that they may or may not have experienced while here; it's the experience of loving and being loved. They refer to the entire experience of finding love and losing love, giving and receiving love, and being loved in ways that were both good and bad as being the only things that matter and are worth remembering from their time here on earth.

CHAPTER
21

The Reward That Awaits Us

"*W*hy did God allow this to happen?" When suffering comes into our lives, it's easy to lose faith, especially when it touches children, vulnerable animals, the aging, the weak, and us. "How can God stand by and watch?" I've been asked.

Instead of coming across as caring, God appears to enjoy our misery, wanting us to kneel, pray, and beg for mercy, but in the end seemingly blind to our pain and deaf to our pleas. I've sat with many people who were afraid to admit that they were angry with this God, because they were afraid that even more punishment would come down on them from Heaven.

I remember a college professor, who had a PhD in philosophy, teaching that suffering had no meaning whatsoever. According to the souls, he'll find out differently once he crosses over to the Other Side. I cannot stress this enough, because I hear the souls reassuring their loved ones over and over again, "What we think of as painful now will have meaning when we're able to see it from their point of view." Not only that, but we'll go so far as to celebrate the fact that we went through it to begin with. In addition, they insist that *all* suffering we go through, especially if we endure it as well as we can, is rewarded by the Eternal Light of Love.

There's a story about a king who had to leave his kingdom to conduct business elsewhere. Before he did, he informed his best friend that he was leaving him in charge of his kingdom. You might think his friend would be overjoyed, but he wasn't. He couldn't be more upset about the king's decision.

"What's wrong?" his wife wanted to know. "This is a great honor our king has bestowed on you!"

"You don't understand," he told his wife. "His advisors will all wonder why I was chosen over them. In time, they will grow resentful about this, and they will torment me!"

Soon after the king left, his advisors did go up to his best friend to ask why their king had picked him instead of them. "I don't know," he told them. The advisors soon became resentful and refused to help the king's friend administer the day-to-day affairs of the kingdom. Then his worst fears were realized, and they turned on him, beating him mercilessly.

When the king returned, he found his friend beaten, bloody, and broken, lying on the ground where the advisors had left him. "What has happened to you, my friend?" the king cried out.

"Your highness," the man responded, "your advisors hated me because you left me in charge while you were gone. They wouldn't help me, wouldn't guide me, eventually attacked me, and left me here."

"How many times did they hit you?" the king asked.

"Forty-two times, your majesty," the man answered, sobbing.

The king turned to his assistant. "Give my friend one piece of gold for each time he was hit," the king demanded and then strode off angrily to confront his advisors. Doing as he was instructed, the assistant counted out forty-two pieces of gold.

The king's friend looked at his new found wealth and cried even harder. "Why? Why? Why didn't they beat me more?"

Misery and sorrow are things we must all endure in our lifetime. The souls say that these are part of our journey here on earth and that we won't appreciate why until our time here is over. I know that it doesn't make any sense and feels impossible to understand while your heart is breaking, but they also reassure us that when it's our time and we see the scope of our life in its entirety, we will understand the whys and wherefores and we will be rewarded for our pain.

Until then, while we are struggling in the midst of the misery we're feeling and the havoc going on in our lives, our mission is to find hope and keep our trust in God intact. According to the souls, the reward was worth every second of pain. The Eternal Light of Love knows exactly what it's doing when it allows suffering to happen, and there is a reason for everything that happens to us here on earth. The question, according to the souls, that we ought to be asking isn't, "Why is this happening?" but "What spiritual lessons can I learn from this?"

Believe me, I know how hard this is, and because of that, I've asked the souls why these things happen. To be honest with you, I still don't have an answer. They say that there are just some things we aren't meant to know while we're here, but *everything* will be answered when we return home again.

One of the most profound things I think that I've learned from the souls is that everything which happens to us while we are here happens for a reason. Every single event that takes place in our life serves a purpose, and that purpose is for our greater good and for the growth of our souls. The souls say all of it plays a part in the creation of a beautiful existence for us in the hereafter. Everything which happens to us here takes place so that we can enjoy time without end there. The Eternal Light of Love adores you too much to shortchange you of the reward that awaits you for having gone through each and every second of suffering you have.

I've sat through countless numbers of sessions, listening to and passing along messages from the souls making it very clear that in their world pain and suffering no longer exist and that struggle is nonexistent. Hurt and grief will one day be a distant memory in the hereafter.

The souls which come through during sessions are vastly different but what they promise is unwavering, "Everything you thought you had lost is found again. Your reward for having lived life on earth with all of its pain, suffering, problems, shortcomings, and grief is life in a world of compassion, joy, peace, and love."

It's a message that helps me to endure what I must live through daily. I hold on with the hope that they are right and that one day what they talk about will be waiting for me when my time here is done. "What a magnificent thing to look forward to," I can't help but think to myself.

Can the souls tell me if there's going to be an answer or miracle to this situation?

Dear Anthony,

I know you remember me and my son from Erie, Pa as we had a reading with you and my grandmother came through very clearly to you. It's been over a year now since my grandmother passed, and I believe my sense of grieving has moved into the acceptance phase, although it was the most painful loss I have ever felt.

You always said I could ask you anything and now I need to ask you something very important with the hope that my grandmother or someone from the Other Side will come through to you. I ask this request with much sincerity.

My best friend is my adoptive mother, who has had me since a baby. She recently had a test at the hospital which revealed several problems and a grim prognosis. It was unexpected and plainly put, the doctors don't know what to do.

My question is . . . Can anyone on the Other Side tell you if there is going to be an answer or a miracle to this or how much time she has left? Can they tell you anything about the situation? She also has a son named Ross on the Other Side that she lost as a stillborn baby. I am asking you to try, out of kindness. I know you do this for a living, but this time I am just asking you to do this out of empathy and compassion alone. Her name is Beverly. I look forward to your response and appreciate your time with utmost respect.
Sharon

I'm asked this sort of plea a lot, so much so that I want to thank you for allowing me to answer your question here.

Recently, an old friend asked me to pray for his mother who was in the hospital in ICU for a heart condition. "I'll pray for you and your family that you find peace during this time and that whatever lessons you need to learn during and after this time, you'll learn them. That'll be my prayer for her too."

My prayer was simply this because the souls have told me that's all any of us can pray for when it comes to these situations so that we might understand, learn, and grow from them.

On a personal note, I was going through a particularly tough time once, and I kept praying that God would make things better. Being a Roman Catholic, I called in the "reserves"—Mary and the saints—to pray with me. Well, you might imagine how upset I was when one of them came to me and said, "Even God can't interfere with what you are going through now, because it would take the lesson away that you need to learn from it; it is one of the lessons you are here to learn before you come back home."

"Are you kidding me?" I cried. "The Source of all creation can't do this one little thing for me?"

"We cannot promise you happiness while you're here. But when you are back home with us . . . " With that she was gone.

My point is that if you were sitting in a session with me, chances are the souls would tell you that your mother is fine. She will receive a reward for the suffering she's going through now when she makes her transition to the hereafter. Her destination is the Other Side of this life where she will experience a reunion with her son Ross, with all those she loved who have gone on before her, and with the Eternal Light of Love. They'll tell you this hoping you'll learn to trust that all is as it's supposed to be. I think one of the most touching and profound things I've heard the souls say, over and over, as they reflect back over their lives and the circumstances that led up to their passing, is, "It all came together so beautifully."

They would probably tell you that the real question you need to ask is, "What lessons of love can I learn from this?"

You said that this came on "unexpectedly." Today, many people will lose their loved ones "unexpectedly." When people come to me for a session, hopping mad with God that this has happened, the soul of their loved one will tell them that the reason God "allowed" this to happen was so that they could learn to love more deeply those who are still here and to forgive more quickly.

Spend meaningful time with God in prayer and meditation. Spend meaningful time with your mother, as much as you can, for as long as you have her here. I suggest that you do the same with your family and all those whom you love. That's based on everything I've heard the souls say about circumstances similar to yours.

I will pray that you find peace during this time and that you'll learn the lessons you are meant to learn for now and for later. That'll be my prayer for your mother as well.

Is my suffering connected to something I did in a past life?

I was told that someone who takes his own life isn't able to move on and that he is stuck in this place called "purgatory." I've never believed that. It didn't make any sense to me.

I do wonder, though, whether the lesson we are here to learn is somehow connected to the pain we feel at the suicide of a loved one. Is it possible that in a past life I took my own life, and therefore I must experience the same pain I caused others?
Donna

Your question reminded me of one I had received from a woman who had seen a medium after her son had committed suicide. She was told that in a *previous* life she and her son were both soldiers in World War I. They were allies fighting in a trench when she was wounded. Her son tried to carry her out of the trench to safety, and she died in his arms.

After he died, while they were both in the hereafter, they made a soul contract that they would come back, and as her son, he would commit suicide so that she would feel the kind of pain he felt when she died in his arms. Needless to say, she left the medium's home in a daze and stayed that way for four months until she came to see me. Even though she didn't tell me what had happened during her session with this medium, her son did.

When her son came through, he was actually laughing so much at what she had been told that she started laughing herself. The relief that this woman felt was immense when she found out that her son

hadn't taken his own life as a way for her to feel what he had suppos-
edly felt when she had died in her arms. He told her that story was
nonsense. For one thing, the whole combat incident never happened.
Even if it had, the souls and the Other Side don't work on a tit-for-tat
basis. "You hurt me, so now we'll both go back to earth in order that
you get to feel the hurt I felt when I commit suicide."

Whatever pain you may have caused others on a previous journey
here will be experienced by you during your life review after you have
crossed over. Having gone through firsthand the suffering you have
caused others, you will get to work on repairing whatever damage
you have caused as part of your spiritual journey on the Other Side in
a place of peace, free of guilt and shame. You will accept what you
have done and you will make amends. You are here to learn a new set
of lessons—none of which have to do with recreating in your own life
the suffering you have inflicted on others in a previous life.

Can those who died in the Twin Towers remember their passing?

Anthony,
I wanted to get in touch with you on the anniversary of 9/11 but needed to
wait for another posting in order to ask my question. (I went to your Web
site but didn't see the option to comment.) Have any souls come through
that were in the Twin Towers on that day and can they recall their passing
as the buildings came down? Most people worry about their suffering and
how fast crossing over takes place. RSVP when you can. Please and thank
you for sharing your gift :-)
Mike

Thanks for the question, Mike!

The way the process works, at least with me, is that I'm like a telephone. In order for the communication to take place, there has to be a
soul who wants to communicate with someone still here; that someone here needs to be willing to receive the messages, and then I act as
the instrument to pass the messages along. In other words, I usually
don't get bombarded by souls chatting with me for no reason.

Because I was in Denver at the time of this tragedy, I didn't get a lot of people reaching out to me as I would have if I had been living in New York. I did one session in which a man was coming through for his daughter, talking about all sorts of people whom she had no idea who they were. That's when he let me know he was on one of the planes that had crashed into one of the towers.

Generally speaking, based on the innumerable sessions I've done, I can tell you this— death ends all suffering and fear. If someone were in one of the towers and died as it fell, whatever fear they experienced would have ceased once they passed from this life into the next. As far as how quickly they would have crossed over, it would have been only a moment. In fact, I've heard many times that death is so quick that the souls say they didn't realize they had "died" until they saw those who had gone before them.

They think of their passing as, "I was there. Now I'm here." As one soul said, "I didn't die. I simply changed addresses." In the case of souls who transitioned in one of the towers, I can imagine them saying, "I was running as fast as I could on the staircase . . . the next thing I knew I was reunited with my loved ones whom I thought were dead!"

Finally, when souls talk about suffering during a session, they speak of it the way you or I would remember a distant memory. They remember it, but they don't experience it. It's talked about with an attitude that sounds like, "Oh yeah . . . that . . . "

22

Love Never Dies

You might be surprised to hear that one of the things which souls speak about a great deal is the subject of relationships. The reason they have so much to say is because, for many, love relationships are an important part of a soul's time here on earth. Two people meet, fall in love, and become part of one another's journey while they're here, and the souls will talk about it as being one of the most beautiful aspects of their earthly journey.

People come into our lives for basically a couple of different reasons—to influence our lives or for us to affect theirs in some way. The souls say that we may be a teacher to some and a student to others, but that most don't realize until they've returned to the hereafter that it was part of the plan all along. These relationships were "made in Heaven," because they were an indispensable part of the design for the journeys of both souls while they were here on earth. But they are quick to remind us that our journey here has everything to do with our life when we return to the hereafter.

Because of that, we will form bonds with others that will last the test of time. There will be on-earth relationships here that were prearranged before we incarnated to test us, our beliefs about others, and our trust in others. Possibly, and most importantly, the lesson we learn is to forgive which allows us to discover our very ability to continue love in spite of the hurt we feel.

The souls understand this principle since they have lived here themselves. They know, from personal experience, that we might give our hearts to people who will turn their backs on us and take their love away. They understand the pain we feel because they've felt it. We may never understand why. They may leave for reasons that they don't understand either. But the souls insist that *everything* which happens in our lives comes full circle, and what we don't understand now will be understood eventually. Until then, we're forced to move forward as best we can, often making decisions based on what we fear instead of what we know.

The souls say that it's during these times when we need to trust, understand, and *believe* that everything has a reason and that out of the pain comes real potential for growth and insight. It takes everything we have at times to keep going when our heart is breaking, but the truth is that we can be better people after the pain and rejection of a relationship ending. The souls will tell you that your journey is still filled with plenty of opportunities to find new love and to share your love with someone new—when the time and the conditions are right.

I've noticed this especially when I'm talking to someone who has lost a loved one. He seems to lose all fear of loss. Because of this, I've met people who are no longer living their lives from a place of fear. The worst that can happen has happened to them. They understand that their life here isn't forever, will end, and even look forward to the day death comes to call them home. I remember having a discussion about this with a friend of mine who insisted no one ever gets over his fear of death. The next day I was doing a session with a woman in her seventies. I asked her if she feared death after having lost so many of her loved ones. I'll never forget her answer: "Oh, honey, if I don't go soon, I'm going to grab a shovel and dig a grave for myself."

It's been my experience that once people have gone through the loss of a loved one, they often lose their fear of loss, period. That's any loss whatsoever. I've also seen that if they can understand their pain, they can survive it and keep putting one foot in front of the other in the face of their agony. It's a hard, but one of the most important lessons we can learn while we're here the souls say—once we experience our worst fears, they no longer have any control over our lives.

It's my hope, and the souls' hope as well, that reading this book helps you understand what the souls desperately want to you know— that the ending of anything in our lives is nothing to fear or dread. Even death is not the end. It's a doorway to a fresh and magnificent new life for you and your loved ones.

I feel like God has forsaken me.

Hi Anthony,
I am very grateful for you.
For the last nine months I have been in sheer agony since the man whom I love, whom I lived with for four years, has left me for his ex-girlfriend. My life has been a mess from the beginning with a very dysfunctional and emotionally unstable family and a life that has constantly denied me peace and the love that I seek.

The last nine months I had hoped that things would get better, that I would learn what God wanted me to learn, and that he would return. Now within the span of those nine months my boyfriend and his ex-girlfriend have decided to get married.

We have never had any issues and we both were very happy. He just said that his feelings have changed though he still loved me. His ex-girlfriend dumped him five years ago after a [dispute] with both families.

I feel very suicidal as I really can't wake up and live like this. I am so disappointed with my life and how it has turned out. All my life I have lived according to the will of God and how my parents have taught me to be. I feel like God has forsaken me. I am twenty-five years old, and I am still just a waitress. I hate my job [because] I always get mental torture from there. My mother hates me, and so I really have no one to talk to who understands what my guy meant to me as he used to give me all the support I needed.

I am going through blogs to validate for myself that it is okay for me to go if I want. I don't belong here anymore. I have sacrificed enough. I can't deal with taking my soul mate away without a proper reason. I really appreciate your taking the time to read this!
Nina

First of all, I want to thank you and commend you for reaching out in your pain. I had to give a great deal of thought to what I needed to say and to wait for the souls to give me an answer from their perspective.

Every once in a while I'll hear from someone who, in her grief, has lost her desire to live. If this is you, the souls have been stubbornly demanding that I share this with you.

According to the souls, the most important lesson that they learn is how much they are loved—not just by God and the souls who have gone before them, but also by those they left behind as well. They talk about being humbled by the love and concern, as well as the high regard others had for them, while they were still here. They say it never occurred to them how much they'd be missed after they had crossed over.

They want you to know that one day you'll be reunited in a world where the pain of loss and feelings of hopelessness and disillusionment do not exist. Until then, do not forget that there are those who love you in the here and now. One of the lessons you're to learn when you feel like shutting down and shutting people out is that *YOU MATTER.*

God and the souls want you to know that you are loved much more than you realize. Finding the courage to open yourself to the love available to you *now,* while you're still here grieving, is another lesson you're being asked to learn. And it is not just the love of your family and friends, but the kindness shown to you by someone who might be just passing through your life.

One of the things that I've learned while doing this work and listening to the souls who have completed their own life journey is that everything happens to us for a reason and for our own spiritual growth. That is everything—the positive events in our lives as well the painful ones.

It's been said that "all healing occurs outside of our comfort zone." I believe that this is especially true when it comes to affairs of the heart. The souls know that our lives can seemingly turn on a dime for seemingly no reason. But they are constantly saying that everything comes full circle, and what doesn't seem to make any sense now will make sense eventually.

While the end of love sometimes feels as though it's the end of our lives, our hearts continue to beat after being broken. What we don't know now, the souls assure us, we will learn later—the pain that rejection makes us feel, which we think will never end, does end and that we will be better people for having gone through the ordeals we do.

The souls would also say to you, "There are lessons for you to learn right where you are, but keep looking at the road ahead of you. Keep putting one foot in front of another. When you lose your fear that you'll never be loved again, you'll lose the fear that you're not loveable."

The fact that we are lovable and loved more than we ever realized while we're here is, according to the souls, the most important lesson they've learned on the Other Side. They talk about how surprised they were at how highly they were thought of, even by people they weren't aware of.

Here's something I'd like you to do to help illustrate this point—

Name two gold medal winners in the 2008 Olympics.

Name four people who have received the Pulitzer Prize.

Name one coach in the NBA Hall of Fame.

Name one person who received the Congressional Medal of Honor last year.

Now—

Name two teachers who have made a significant impact on your life.

Name four authors, poets, or musicians who have written something you treasure.

Name someone who taught you values, discipline, or persistence.

Name *one* person who would stand by you in your darkest hour.

Which group has had the most lasting impact on your life?

I guarantee you that if I asked enough people *someone* would name you as the answer to the "darkest hour" question.

And you don't think you're loveable?

Think again. When the time and the circumstances are right, some-one will come into your life once again who will love you as you are.

CHAPTER
23

Soul Mates/Sole Mates

*W*henever someone asks me why the souls reach out to talk to us, my typical answer is love. Love for us seems to require them to let us know that they are not only happy in their new life, but that they also want us to be happy while we're still here.

When I did a reading for "Cookie," she was hoping to find out that her one true love had survived death and was still with her.

"I have a man here with an 'R' name," I told her. "Do you take the name Robert, living or deceased?"

Even over the phone, I could hear Cookie's excitement when I had asked her that. "Yes, that's the name of the person I was hoping to hear from."

"Good news, then. He's reaching out to you from the Other Side. He's showing me hearts and flowers, my symbol for romance. You two were a couple, am I correct?"

"Yes," she said, a little more quietly. I could hear her starting to sob.

"I've got to tell you. He's got a great sense of humor," I told Cookie. "He's teasing you."

"That's my Robert, all right!" Cookie said excitedly. "He *loved* to tease me!"

Robert passed on evidence of their life together, their plans for their future, and how they were tragically cut short when he was diagnosed with a terminal disease. Then he dropped a bomb that I knew Cookie wasn't prepared to hear even before I said it.

"Cookie, Robert wants me to tell you that it's okay for you to fall in love again. He wants you to be happy. He wants you to love again."

"No!" Cookie screamed and cried into my ear. "That's not Robert! I don't believe it! He wouldn't say that! We were *soul mates*! Why would tell you he wants me to fall in love with someone else! You tell him I won't do it! I won't!"

"You just did," I told Cookie.

"We both knew this would go over like a lead balloon," I told Robert.

When it comes to the idea of "soul mates," the souls have a great deal to say, and it may not be what you may think they would say about it, but it's surprisingly down-to-earth.

When most people think of their soul mate, what they're referring to is someone in whom they have a powerful, magnetic attraction to. It's someone whom we can communicate with verbally or without saying a single word. Our soul mate is our one and only, the one person we are destined to be with, and the one whom we must persistently search for if we're lucky enough to find him or her. Romantic isn't it? According to the souls, it's also wrong.

To understand what they see as "soul mates," we have to start with the idea that we each have been here more than once before. We come here to learn a specific lesson that enables us to grow spiritually, understand our divinity, and deepen our relationship with the Eternal Light of Love.

The lessons are as varied as the souls themselves who choose to come here. The lesson might be to learn humility, serve humanity, experience wealth, poverty, or giving and receiving love. Whatever the reason, we decide to return here only after a great deal of time spent on the Other Side with people whom we lived with on earth— other souls who were our parents, grandparents, siblings, children, and others whose lives we touched, and who touched our lives here on earth. Whatever the association we might have had with someone in an earlier incarnation here on earth, we could very well have different relationships and connections this go round. Adversaries become lovers, parent and child becomes student and teacher, brothers and sisters become mortal enemies.

Upon arriving here, our memory of the Other Side and the lesson we came here to learn are wiped out, but we are still connected to those we were with in a previous life and in the hereafter before we returned here. It's a connection we feel that can't be explained by earth's standards, because it's spiritual.

So even though Cookie's idea that because she and Robert were "soul mates," at least according to the New Age definition of it, she couldn't, and wouldn't, find and fall in love with someone else. Robert, now in the hereafter, sees it in an entirely different light. To him, and to all of the souls, while it may or may not be in the setting of a romantic relationship at a very basic and spiritual level, your soul mate is someone with whom you were connected to, are connected to, and will be connected to for eternity.

Does this mean that he doesn't love me anymore?

Hi, Anthony!
It's my first opportunity to listen to your radio show. I thoroughly enjoyed it and hope to catch future shows.

I've a question about something stated in my reading with you back on May 30th @ 1:00 pm. You stated that my Robert said to you he wants me to "move on," and that you thought I wouldn't like to hear this. Of course you were correct.

Does Robert's "request" mean he doesn't love me anymore? The Robert I knew and loved (still do very much today) would never request that of me. I cannot believe that's what he'd like me to do! Does this request mean that he WILL NOT be there to meet me when I cross over as we had talked about when he was still here in the physical world?!?!

I've sat for one entire month with these questions, crying and worrying that I'll never see him again OR worse, much worse, never experience our love, his love for me again.

*Please, Anthony, help me understand what's behind this absolutely ab-
surd "request." I can't and won't believe that's what Robert REALLY wants
me to do. I'm all confused.*
Cookie

As soon as I read this, the souls compared it to a woman having
one child and saying that she didn't want another one because she
might stop loving the first one as much as she does now.

Your question reminded me of something someone I knew told me
at a party over thirty years ago. She was a movie buff and said that
when she was a child and saw someone killed in a movie or on television, she thought that he had really died and would never be able to
appear in another movie or television show again. She said she often
wondered, "Why would anyone want a job like that?"

At that time, since she was in her twenties and a lot more mature
and wise, she realized that the actors were playing roles. She understood then what, when she was young, she had thought was an "ab-
surd" occupation.

One thing we need to remember is that when we leave the Other
Side to come here, we do so in order to learn lessons in love. In order
to do so, we take on "roles," so to speak, and design the circumstances
that we believe will be the most beneficial to help us learn these lessons.

While Robert may have been your "one true love" in this life, you,
according to the souls, could very well have been his grandfather, and
he your granddaughter, in a previous one. Or he could have been
your sister, and you his brother. You two might even have been mortal
enemies.

After we cross over, we let go of the need for these guises and become who we really are once again. That doesn't mean that just because he isn't playing the character of "Robert" in this lifetime
anymore, that he no longer loves you as well. When you cross over,
you will know him by the love he had for you here and throughout
eternity. He will know you by the love you have for him.

So when Robert told you that it was okay for you to move on with
your life, what he was saying wasn't that he doesn't love you, but that
he wants you to live your life to the fullest, and if that means you fall

in love again, with someone else . . .

As I write this, I can hear Robert laughing and calling you "silly" for thinking that he would stop loving you, especially from the Other Side where love is unconditional.

"Do you really think that if you fell in love again that I would stop loving you or not be here to welcome you when you come back home?" he's asking. "I'd be happy for you! Our love for one another is eternal. Nothing can ever change that."

He's where he is because he's learned the lessons of love he was supposed to learn. You are still here because you have lessons you still need to learn. When he told you during your reading that he wants you to be open to falling in love again, it's because that's part of the lessons you're here to learn. It's not because he no longer loves you. It's because he loves you more now than he was able to when he was still here.

Why do we feel an instant connection to some people?

Anthony, when you meet someone and feel an instant attraction to his energy . . . a feeling of familiarity . . . could that mean you're meeting someone who is traveling in your "circle," the folks you are supposed to meet up with? It doesn't happen often . . . but it is quite profound when it does. You hear something in his voice that is comforting . . . like a sweet memory . . . but you know you've never met before.
Kathi

I spoke with a woman recently, and while we were talking to each other, I couldn't help but feel I knew her. The way she was looking at me I could tell she was thinking the same thing.

I saw her again later that day and she said, "Hi, Anthony, do you remember me? I'm Wendy!" It was then I realized why she looked so familiar. We knew one another but hadn't seen each other in almost seven years! We spent a few minutes catching up and sharing old familiar memories. "Aren't you the one who . . . ?"

After that second meeting that day, we never saw each other again. I'm telling you this story because it applies to what you're asking. The truth is that our soul mates are *everywhere*.

Another truth is that just because someone is a soul mate, it does not mean we will necessarily build a relationship with them or even around them during this lifetime. Sometimes we recognize them as strangers we pass during the course of our day, but we can't shake the feeling that we knew that person somewhere, and in some way we don't remember. The French word for this is *déjà vu* which means, "already seen." The hunch we feel that we know someone we haven't met, is because we have met, we've "already seen" one another—in another lifetime, in another context, on another road of our journey. In any case, the feelings we had for that person are still there. Other times, we are fortunate enough to have that "soul mate" in our lives and have the chance to get to know and love them here. Either way, the connection we have with those souls we share a community with on the Other Side and here on earth doesn't end, never changes, and never dies—it endures just as we do—from this life into the next.

What happens if my spouse dies and I remarry?

Anthony, I've always been curious about this. What if one spouse dies and the other remarries . . . what kind of reunion will they have when they die? What about when the second spouse dies as well and all three are reunited? Kim

When you asked this question, the souls reminded me of some sessions I've done. One was with a man whose wife was coming through and told him that she wanted him to fall in love again. "But it's been only ten months," he told me, with tears in his eyes.

"And it may be ten years before you meet someone else, but she's giving you the 'green light' to go ahead and fall in love again."

I did a session for a woman whose mother came through scolding her and her sisters for being angry with their father because he had fallen in love again after her passing. "I don't want him to be alone," she said. "More than anything, I want him to be happy, and you know that he doesn't do well being alone. He's happy. I'm happy for him. Why can't you be happy for him too? He's not being unfaithful to me. I'm the one who brought her to him so they could meet!"

One woman's husband, who had passed away from a massive coronary seven years before, told his wife, "Don't think for a moment that if you meet someone and fall in love with him, you'll be betraying me."

She related this to me that just two days before a mutual friend of hers and her husband mentioned to her, "There's someone I want to introduce you to, but I don't want to betray Jake (her husband)!"

Then there was a session in which I told a woman that the love of her life wanted her to move on and fall in love again. "He'd never tell me that. He wouldn't want me to fall in love with someone else."

"Well, yeah," I said, "he does."

Just recently I did a session with a woman during which I asked, "Were your mother and father divorced?"

"Yes."

"But they've both passed away?"

"Yes."

"Okay, then what your father just said makes sense. He wants you to know that they've reconciled and are 'united' again on the Other Side."

"That's hard to believe," she told me. "They hated each other while they were alive."

I shrugged my shoulders. "They seem to have gotten over that."

Love is the rule, not the exception, in the hereafter. We come here to learn lessons in love so that we can experience more fully the Eternal Light of Love on the Other Side. The souls say that where they are, love reigns supreme. Just as grudges and resentments retard our spiritual growth here, they do the same there as well. So much so that the souls realize very quickly that there's no sense in holding on to anything that isn't love.

Having learned this, they want us to know that every experience we have here serves the purpose of teaching us how to love more deeply, and if part of that journey means that you'll fall in love and remarry, they are all for it!

It's love that unites us here and love will reunite us there. I did a session for a woman who had been married six times, twice to the same man. All of them had passed away, and all of them showed up during the session! Not only did they show up, but they told her that they all knew each other and what brought them together was their love for her.

She told me that she was afraid that they might meet and that there might have been some jealousy or resentment among them. They assured her that it was exactly the opposite. Jealousy is the byproduct of fear, and where there is love, there is no fear. Again, on the Other Side love is the rule, no exceptions.

"So who will be there to greet me when it's my time?" she wondered out loud.

"All of us," was their reply.

We Are Family . . . Forever

As a soul comes closer to earth during a reading, much of its personality comes through in a way that reflects its character while it was here. If your loved one was quiet and long-suffering in this life, the soul will come across the same way from the next. If he was rebellious and high-strung, then he will typically come across the same way during the session.

I was doing a reading for a young woman named Michelle whose grandmother came through. As the reading progressed, her grandmother came across to me in a way that I found funny. This wasn't the way her granddaughter remembered her though, and she began to have her doubts that it was really her grandmother I was hearing from.

Now, I always do the best I can to deliver the messages I'm receiving as closely to the way they're being given to me as possible, but I'm not 100% accurate nor do I claim to be. So when I got a piece of evidence wrong, I said to Michelle, "Your grandmother just smacked me on the forehead with the palm of her hand and said, 'Get it right, psychic boy!'"

Michelle burst out laughing and said, "Now *that* sounds like the grandmother I knew and loved!" That was when she admitted to me, for the first time, her misgivings about whether or not I really was communicating with her grandmother. In addition she did admit that her Italian grandmother could be charming when she wanted to be.

Another time I did a face-to-face session with a mother, Kim, and her daughter, Resa, during which their husband and father came through. Kim and her husband, Roun, were from Cambodia. Although Kim spoke English perfectly, Resa did most of the talking during the session. "We were wondering if we could ask questions."

"I'd prefer that you don't," I told her. "There are two reasons. One is that even though I'm speaking to you, I'm also listening to whoever is going to come through for you. If they're talking to me while you're asking a question, it might confuse me. The second reason is that in all of the years I've been doing this, I've found that they will tell you what you need to know. In fact, they'll usually answer your questions without you having to ask them."

They nodded their understanding, and I began the session.

I began with my usual prayer, "May the Lord bless me and keep me. May He cause His face to shine upon me; may He grant me accuracy and peace during this session with Kim and Resa. If you are standing in the light of God and wish to come forward to speak to Kim and Resa, please do so now."

Roun's energy was vibrant and strong. He struck me as the kind of person who, when he was still here, knew no strangers. "The first thing he's showing me is a rosary. Whenever I see that I know I'm supposed to acknowledge someone who prays *a lot.*"

That would be my husband, Kevin," Resa said. "He prays a lot."

"Then your husband must be praying for your father too, if your father is acknowledging your husband in this way," I said to her.

"He does," she nodded with tears in her eyes.

The next thing I saw, psychically, was a golden Buddha. "You're not Catholic though. You're Buddhist." They both nodded, "Our whole family is," Resa explained. "Except for my husband, he's Catholic."

I saw saffron colored robes. I looked at Kim, "Your husband was a monk at one point in his life." She nodded again.

Then I saw him feeding chickens. "He raised chickens back in Cambodia too?" I asked.

Both of them grew wide eyed and said loudly, "Yes!"

"Now he's telling me that he wore sandals *all of the time.*"

Resa laughed. "Yes, even in the dead of winter."

That's when I realized that Roun's sense of humor extended even to himself. "He says that his feet weren't the easiest to look at."

Both of the ladies squealed with laughter again. "His feet were *ugly,*" Resa explained. "If you would have seen them, you would have said he had ugly feet too!" she laughed, smiling with tears in her eyes.

"He wants to talk about the fried rice he cooked."

"Fried rice was his go-to meal," Resa told me, laughing again, along with her mother. "And it was gross! Wasn't it?" she asked looking at her mother, who nodded. I was really starting to enjoy Roun's self-deprecating sense of humor.

Looking at Kim, I said, "He wants to tell you that he loves you to the moon and back."

Kim started crying. "Just last night I was looking at the moon and telling him I loved him."

"He loved the water." Kim and Resa nodded. "He is showing he loved to fish too."

"Yes!" Resa said.

"He didn't go fishing as much as he liked, but he did love fishing," Kim explained.

"He wants you to know that on the Other Side, he lives by a river and is able to fish from it now. The souls refer to where they are as "the Other Side," because it takes the religious part out of the equation. Buddhists would call where they are 'Nirvana.' Christians refer to it as 'Heaven.' Muslims call it 'Paradise.' The souls refer to it as 'the Other Side'" because it's inclusive to all, no matter what their religion or faith was—even if they didn't have one when they were here." Kim nodded that she understood.

"I have to tell you something, and he's making me feel as though I really need to get this across. On the Other Side, he not only lives near a river, but he lives in a cabin."

"He always wanted to live in a cabin!" Resa said. "He was always saying that he wanted to own a cabin in the mountains, and we could live there. We would tell him, 'Go ahead and get a cabin, but there's no way we're going up there with you. We don't like the outdoors the way you do.'"

I laughed and said, "I'm the same way. My idea of roughing it is a 'bran muffin' in the morning. Anyway, he wants me to tell you that he'll be waiting for you in his cabin when it's time for you to join him on the Other Side."

Looking at Kim I said, "He doesn't want you to worry. He'll be there to greet you when you cross over." She nodded she understood with tears in her eyes.

When the session ended, Resa said, "One of the questions we had was whether or not he had already reincarnated by now."

Does marriage exist in Heaven?

Anthony, I have a question for you. After you and your spouse pass when you reach heaven, are you still like you were on earth as a married couple and do you know each other when you were on earth together?
Mary Ann

Great question!

As the subtitle of my first book suggests, "death is not the end of life, love, or relationships." But does that mean that the relationships we have with people remain the same on the Other Side?

Does that mean that our relationships remain unchanged? The answer is no.

Let's look at the flip side of that question. Do the people we hold grudges against here mean that we'll hold the same grudge against them in the hereafter? Again, the answer is no.

When we're holding a grudge, the challenge is to learn how to forgive. When we learn that, we grow spiritually. What you don't forgive here, you'll have to let go of during your life review without the benefit of having learned the lesson it contained.

The relationships we have here serve to help us grow spiritually so that when we return back home, our life on the Other Side reflects how well we learned the lessons we came to earth to learn.

Having said that, the purpose of marriage in this life is that we vow to one another that we'll provide a safe haven for each other to grow and discover who we are in the eyes of God, "until death do us part." There's no need for marriage on the Other Side because we are seen and accepted for who we really are, and our marriage here has served its purpose.

Will we know one another in the hereafter? Absolutely. We will know and love one another in a way that isn't possible in this life.

How do families stay together in the hereafter?

Dear Anthony,

I finished your book. I think it's fantastic. I really hope you write another one. You are a great writer.

You didn't go into reincarnation in your book. I've often wondered how families keep together on the Other Side when we could have had different relationships in different lives.

For example, my granddad in this life could have been my sister in another. Which 'family' do we meet with? I get the feeling that each family is probably happening at the same time in its own dimension or we progress as a group for as long as we need after one life and then all reincarnate around the same time. Who knows?

Ian

The souls say that we live in communities with our loved ones on the Other Side. We decide to come to this plane of existence to learn the lessons we need to learn in order to experience The Eternal Light of Love, or God, more fully.

We also plan what the ideal circumstances will be and pick roles we will assume while we're here in order to learn these lessons. So your grandfather in this life may very well have been your sister in another, but what is important isn't the role, but the love we learn.

When I say that "death isn't the end of life, love, or relationships," the "relationship" I'm speaking of is the love we have for one another. When someone comes through during a reading and identifies himself as your "mother," it's because that's how you knew that soul in this life. Once you cross, you'll recognize one another by the love you experienced for the other one, no matter what the sex was during that life.

The souls also say that on the Other Side we are inclined to stay close to the souls that you were close to here. This seems to be the reason why we may have parents in this lifetime different from those in the last one, and our brother or sister could be a parent in our next life.

While it does seem that we've always been with the same people from the beginning, it may also be that we meet different people along the way. As we craft our lives, we try to live in such a way as to best learn the lessons we came here to acquire; other souls can play an important part by highlighting and enhancing our lives at specific points on our journey.

According to the souls, we spend a lot of time on the Other Side before deciding to come back here, because this plane of existence is so hard. But it's also the easiest way to gain knowledge of the lessons we need to learn. Still, some souls have emphatically told me, "I'm *never* doing that again."

The reasons for that feeling vary, but the common reason seems to be that it's easy to become waylaid from our original purpose for coming here. I don't have to tell you that while we're here, we're faced with temptations, distractions, conflicts, as well as positive aspects. So some souls will say that they'll continue their journey and work out their lessons and growth in the hereafter even if it does take longer . . . much longer than it would if they had come here.

While most souls, such as you and I, have chosen to come here to learn what we need to advance spiritually, we may have loved ones who say, "I don't want to go to earth to be tested in the flesh again. I'll just stay here and learn what I need as long as it takes." Even so, you will be once again reunited with the souls you love and are close to on the Other Side.

What do the souls say about reincarnation?

Hi, Anthony,
Having read through some of the posts [on your website] and having no-

ticed before that your book is connected to A.R.E., I am wondering if you have read any of the Cayce readings. Many years ago I spent a lot of time going through the Cayce readings. At the time I was more in search of alternative healing ideas.

Have you ever had a soul speak of a previous life with the person asking for a reading from you?

Once again, thanks, Anthony.

Jeff

It does come up, and people like to talk about "contracts" from past lives and such. I have a friend who was told by some kind of psychic type that the difficulties she's having with her husband in this life are the result of difficulties that they had in previous lifetimes and the spiritual contracts they have between them.

The souls have a very different take on it. What the souls stress is that we are all here to learn a specific lesson. Whoever you were in a previous life, whatever relationships you had with others in the life, you learned the lessons you were supposed to learn. What is important now are the lessons you chose to come here to learn in this lifetime.

They also say that you, and everyone in your life, come here as a community, and you eventually return to a community. So there's no danger of you going home, hoping to reunite with someone you loved here, only to be told, "Damn, she returned to earth ten minutes ago. If only you'd crossed over a few minutes earlier . . . "

Interestingly, I read that even the Buddha himself discouraged his followers from contemplating questions such as, "What was I in the past? What shall I be in the future?" because he explained that asking those questions leads only to self-doubt, fear, and distraction.

Based on what I've heard them say over innumerable readings, the souls couldn't agree more.

Can a soul be here and in the hereafter at the same time?

Anthony, I have a question that I'm hoping you can give me a little insight on . . . My husband passed away five years ago, but he had a child that was born six months after he died. Every time I see his son, I see that there is so

much similarity between them. He seems to have knowledge and talents way beyond his years. These facts make me wonder if somehow he has an actual piece of my husband's soul within him. Now you have done a reading, so I know that my husband is in Heaven. My question is this . . . is it possible for a soul to be in two different planes of existence at the same time?
Stacy

When I read your question, I remembered a reading I did for a woman during which her father came through for a couple of different reasons. One of them was that when her father pulled his energy away, she asked me, "Are you able to communicate with someone who has incarnated?" My first thought was to answer, "Well, I'm talking to you aren't I?" but before I did, it hit me what she was asking.

Her mother and father, as well as a few other souls, came through during her session. She told me before we began that she had talked with a number of mediums previously. Apparently, one of them told her that either her mother or father had already reincarnated and was back here on the physical plane. I'm assuming that she was told this about her father since he passed away before her mother who had crossed over only recently.

So she was wondering if everything I was telling her was being communicated to me by a soul that now inhabits the body of a young child.

I told her what I had been told only the night before—if a soul decides to come back (reincarnate) in order to learn lessons that will enable it to diminish its sense of separateness from God, it is done after a great deal of time has passed and after it has reunited with all of the souls of its loved ones. In other words, the chances of her crossing over and asking, "Where's my mom?" and being told, "Oh, you just missed her; she left ten minutes ago. If only you'd have passed sooner," are slim to none.

According to the souls, reincarnation does happen, but only after a great deal of time, and thought.

There is one last thing regarding this reading. After establishing that her father was a scientist while he was alive, I asked her, "Was your father a physicist?"

"Yes," she said, stunned. "It's amazing that you were able to nail that about him."

"Not really," I told her. "He's saying that he's become friends with Albert Einstein and that they spend a lot of time together talking."

I then asked her, "Do you really think he's in any big hurry to come back here when he has to opportunity to sit on a recliner relaxing and chatting with Albert Einstein about God?" We both laughed.

I have to say it was a real kick in the pants to be able to even talk about Albert Einstein, let alone see him with the soul of this woman's father!

According to the souls I've heard from, they say that there is only "one soul per customer." So, no, I don't think that there's an actual piece of your husband within your son.

As to what is happening with your son, there is an idea that when we pass away, we while away the time "resting in peace," floating on clouds, etc. The souls say that *nothing* could be further from the truth. They say that compared to here, it is the "vacation they never had," but it's because everything they do is done in love, joy, and peace.

They also say that the end of this life is not the end of our spiritual journey. It continues on the Other Side as well.

After our life review we continue our spiritual journey, and part of that is often guiding those we love along their journey here on earth. So while your son doesn't have an "actual piece" of your husband within him, he apparently has your husband as his "guide."

Many people believe that their guides are someone who has nothing to do with them, like a guy who was an Eskimo and had lived in the early 1900s. He called himself "Big Joe" or an Indian chief. Again, according to the souls, that just isn't the case. They are *typically* someone who knew and loved you and are interested in helping you along your journey while you're still here, although that may not always be the case.

At one point, for several months, two of my guides were men I hadn't met here on earth, but in a reading. They were the father and uncle of a woman I became friends with years after the session. Because I helped her, they told me that they wanted to help me. They accompanied me until I completed a very difficult phase of my journey, and then they acknowledged my accomplishment. I haven't heard from either of them since.

So when you see your son growing and developing in ways that remind you of your husband, know that it's his father doing what he would have done were he still here . . . being a daddy to his son.

CHAPTER

25

The Skeleton in All of Our Closets

The souls say that suicide is the skeleton in all of our closets. I'm writing this chapter from the perspective of my experience as a medium who has received messages sent to loved ones by the souls who have taken their own lives, and not as a counselor or therapist (this is what is known as a "disclaimer.")

The sister of someone I knew told her roommate that she was going out for a drive. A couple of hours later the roommate found my friend's sister still in their garage with her car running. Even though I wasn't a "medium" at the time, I said, "I'm sure she's found the peace in the next life that she didn't find here."

If there's one constant we can count on while we're going through our journey here on earth, it's that nothing stays the same. The souls say we come here to transform ourselves, but life can bring some people to a better understanding of who they are and their purpose, while it'll bring others to their knees, making them feel fragile and unable to cope. This is where the souls can be extremely helpful, now that they are able to look back and can see the purpose for everything that happens to us. They understand that the whole lot has a beginning and an end with a clear intention which connects them both. But when you're up to your ass in alligators, it's easy to forget that the reason you're in the swamp to begin with is to drain it. Life becomes too much to bear, and for some, it leads them to decide to continue their journey back home to peace and serenity.

It's been my experience working with those who have lost someone who has died by his own hand that they deal with feelings of failure, humiliation, and even blame from friends and relatives. Survivors have told me that they blame themselves for not seeing any "warning signs."

They come to me, as a medium, hoping to hear from their loved one the answer to the question "Why?" The answer the souls give is often that they simply didn't have the strength any longer to continue in this life. Once they crossed over the threshold between this life and the next, they were able to see their problems for what they really were—opportunities to grow spiritually. Their life review showed them that they *did* have alternative answers which they didn't see, or even seemed possible, while they were still here. These answers could have helped them work through their issues.

On occasion, people who have lost loved ones have come to me for a reading hoping to receive "permission" to take their own lives, thinking that it's a solution to their problems or a way to speed up their reunion with their loved ones on the Other Side. I want to make something very clear—I've never heard a soul say during one of my readings that this was an acceptable solution to the problems that we face here. They say that they still have to learn on the Other Side what they didn't learn here by cutting their lives short.

"Doesn't God punish people who commit suicide?" I've been asked. I'm happy to say, "Absolutely not. In fact, God seems to hold them closer in His love."

What was my son's life review like?

Anthony,
My son died of suicide, depressed, and addicted. What was his life review

like? Was he instantly healed of those issues or does he have something to
do before he finds peace? Is he okay now?
Kathi

First of all I want to thank you for having the courage to ask this question. As I said before, suicide is the skeleton in all of our closets. I'm going to answer your questions from the point of view of my experience as a medium, dealing with suicides, and not as a counselor or therapist.

Whenever I have a session during which a soul who has crossed himself over comes through, one of the first things he wants to assure his loved ones of is the fact that he is at peace and safely in the arms of God. Whatever torment caused him to choose to end his live here no longer exists for him on the Other Side. Souls have said that the Eternal Light of Love understands that those who take their own lives didn't want to die as much as they wanted only to end their torment.

These souls simply don't have the strength or desire to continue any longer in this life than they have to. Many of these precious souls have said during my sessions with them that even though they functioned in a way that allowed them to get through the day "normally," their mental torment was a huge factor in their decision.

Your son was not judged for what he did nor was he condemned to "hell." It's quite the opposite, actually. Based on what the souls have said to me before, he may have been taken to a place where he could reflect, and heal, from the anguish that he had endured and had thought there was no way out of. During this time and in this place, there is no one to get in his face, so to speak. His companions during this period will be small creatures such as birds, rabbits, kittens, puppies, cats, and dogs as well as other animals that are there to help the healing process by offering unconditional love to souls such as your son's.

Only when he is strong enough, will relatives, friends, and guides appear to help him understand and learn what he needs to know to continue on his spiritual journey. Christ also appears, not as a judge, but more as a consoler, helping him through his hurt and confusion over what he's done.

God doesn't make mistakes, but understands when we do. The souls have told me over and over that suicide is a mistake on the part of those who have ended their time here in this way. It's a blunder they committed in their confusion. They take complete responsibility for what they've done and insist that there's nothing for their loved ones, who are still here, to feel guilty about.

Finally, your son would want you to know that you *will be* reunited with him on the Other Side, when you've learned the lessons you're here to learn, and not see suicide as a way to speed up the reunion. Until then he will continue to be with you as your "guardian angel," never abandoning you or leaving your side. He will continue doing the best he can to help you understand that everything which happens in this life benefits you in the next—even surviving the tragedy of his suicide.

Are the souls still troubled when they cross over?

I have been asked a question, and you are the go-to-guy. Her question is: If a person has a mental/emotional illness, such as bi-polar disorder or schizophrenia, will his soul also exhibit symptoms of the disorder when he crosses over? I find the question to be interesting. When you are able to respond, I would greatly appreciate it. Thanks!
Ashley

The good news is that when a soul crosses over, whatever mental/emotional disorders that were going on here on earth disappear. The souls assure me that these conditions are simply seen as part of the soul's journey, and a necessity for the lessons they came here to learn.

Some souls will come across talking about the issues they had to deal with while they were here and what they might have done because of them, but it's used only as "evidence" during the session that it's truly them, not because it's still a part of who they are. Still, even when the souls speak of these things, they might remember the circumstances, but they don't seem to remember the feeling of what it was like to experience them. In other words, they may speak of suffering from depression while they were here, but they aren't depressed while they're on the Other Side and don't remember what it was like to feel depressed while they were here!

I've heard the souls insist time and time again that whatever sort of pain we experience here will be a distant memory there and that life there is a reward for having endured our life here. They constantly want to assure us that this is something to look forward to.

Do the souls regret making the mistake of committing suicide?

From what I've read, you say that you've never heard from a soul who took responsibility for ending its own life express regret over what it had done. Yet, you also say that souls discourage their loved ones from doing the same thing, saying that what they did was a mistake.

Is it because suicide is not part of any soul's plan for when they incarnate in the first place?
Mike

First of all, let me just say that while the souls who have crossed over by their own hand don't talk about "regret" with regards to what they did, they understand that it probably wasn't the best decision on their part. Due to the constant confusion in their lives, many, if not all, of those, who pass by their own hand, thought that the decision to end their lives was a good one. These souls are not judged by the Eternal Light of Love but are treated in a very special way because the anguish they went through was to their spirit as cancer is to the physical body.

For that reason, whenever the souls speak of "regret," it's not over anything that they've done, but the things that they didn't do. When they ended their life by their own hand, they also cut short the opportunities to learn from the experiences that life has to offer to us. But as the souls once told me, "When someone doesn't like himself, his soul shrivels up."

A woman named Debbie booked an appointment to see me. Even though she paid for a medium session, she wasn't sure that's what she needed. "I just felt compelled to call you. I don't know why, but it was like the spirits wanted me to talk to you."

The last time I had seen her was probably three years before. Since that time she had divorced a man who was mentally and emotionally abusing her, telling her she wasn't lovable which, unfortunately, she believed. She told me that since her divorce she had tried to take her own life twice in two weeks. The first time she was saved, ironically enough, by her ex-husband. The second time she told me that she knew God was telling her that this wasn't the right thing to do, so she took steps to get help after she took an overdose of pills.

Since she didn't book an appointment to help her with her grief over losing someone she had loved, I felt the souls wanted me to help her deal with her distress over being alive. I shared with her a little of what the souls have told me about suicide, and I thought I'd share the same with you in this post.

Whenever someone comes across who has taken his own life, one of the ways I know is that his energy is as heavy at it gets. After doing a number of readings in which *victims* of suicide come through, I've come to understand that suicide is a disease that slowly erodes the person's will to live. For most of us, when we experience times that make us question how much more we can take, we respond by developing ways of coping until the pain passes or we overcome whatever obstacles are in our way. For these precious souls however, they just don't seem to be able to do that. I don't think it's because of a weakness in their character. In fact, it may be the opposite ... they may just be too good for this world. Whatever the reason, they aren't able to develop the protective barrier around themselves that they need to withstand the trials and tribulations we must all face during our life here. When this happens, they choose to learn the lessons they need in a world of peace.

I have never had a soul that chose this route say that it regretted its decision, but *every one of them* cautioned their loved ones *against* doing the same. Why? Because the lessons are so much easier to learn here.

Darlene wanted to take her own life because she felt unlovable. She married a man who constantly reinforced this belief. The lesson she's meant to learn is that she is lovable. She was created by the Eternal Light of Love who finds her impossible not to love, especially in her darkest moments. If she were successful in either one of her attempts, she would still have to learn why she's lovable, ironically, in an environment in which she is surrounded and supported by God's love. In other words, she'll find herself overwhelmed by love, not knowing why, because she crossed over not believing she was worthy of being loved. Not only that, but she'll have to learn why without the benefit of anyone getting in her face.

What I did with Debbie that night was to have her question whether she truly was unlovable. "I see you the same way God sees all of his children," I told her. "I see you as perfect, just the way you are. What's not to love?" I then helped her find all the reasons she is lovable. She left our appointment shining with joy and hope.

"Besides," I told her, "You still have lessons to learn and to teach others." "How do you know?" she asked me.

"You're still breathing."

He's proud he committed suicide and ruined my life.

I went to a psychic fair yesterday . . . after about an hour of dragging my feet I went to a medium and got a reading. My brother had committed suicide when he was eighteen. I was sixteen. Here is what happened at the reading.

My Grammy came through right away . . . and gave me a hug . . . said something about my left arm? Nothing came to mind. Then . . . yup Mario (my brother). This is very weird and the man said in all of the years he had been doing this never had he relayed this before.

Mario said he is proud of what he did . . . that everyone thought him to be a coward and he finally achieved something. He isn't in Heaven, but he isn't in hell either, said he had lots of lessons to learn still, and that it isn't what he thought it would be.

I am disturbed a bit. I really don't know what to think. The man also said Mario has fond memories of building Legos with me.

It's not very comforting. I feel like I got hit with a baseball bat.
Elizabeth

I am a full-time medium and the author of *Communications from the Other Side: Death Is Not the End of Life, Love, or Relationships.* I was inspired to write my book by a young woman who took her own life.

For a period of about a year, three out of every four readings I did concerned someone who had taken his own life. I learned a lot during

that time, and I'd like to share with you some of what I came to understand from these sessions.

In all the sessions I've done in which someone has come through
like your brother, I have never heard any of those souls say that they
were proud of what they did. By the same token, however, I have
never heard souls say that they regretted what they did either. There
are several reasons for this. One is that they are in a place in which
they're loved unconditionally, despite what they did. They don't
minimize taking their own life, and they don't recommend that their
loved ones do so as well, but they say that at the time they did it they
thought it was their only option.

What I believe your brother would want you to know, if he was
really communicating with you through this "medium," is that he has
found the peace that eluded him here on earth and that he is with
God. I have heard over and over again from these souls that God
holds them close to His heart, understanding the pain that drove them
to do what they do.

In my book I talk about an incident where I was about to do a
group reading, and before anyone arrived, I told my friend Rachel,
who was there to film the session, that there was someone who was
coming to reconnect with a loved one who had committed suicide.
She asked me how I knew, and I told her I could feel the energy of the
soul who did it and it was as heavy as it gets.

Now some mediums may feel this energy and say that the soul is
still depressed over what it did. This just isn't the case. Souls on the
Other Side are at peace, but use this heaviness to let me know what
they did. I believe this may have been what happened in the case of
the person who did your reading: he misinterpreted the feelings he
was getting from your brother.

As far as your brother not being in hell, but not being in Heaven
either, again, I believe it is simply a misinterpretation of what the
medium was receiving on his part. Your brother does have lessons he
needs to learn, but that does not mean he's not at peace nor that he is
unloved by God. All souls are greeted with compassion, love, and understanding, both by the souls on the Other Side and the Eternal Light
of Love.

I hope this helps you find some comfort. The souls come to us during an *authentic* reading from a place of peace, joy, and love. The idea that you left the reading feeling as though you were hit by a baseball bat was certainly not the intent of your brother. It also says to me that what you heard wasn't real.

That being said, if anyone claiming to be a medium tells you that the soul of your loved one is not at peace or is not *unconditionally loved* by God . . . end your time with that person immediately and walk away.

Why shouldn't I take my own life?

Hi Anthony,
If you've never met a soul who regretted its choice for self-deliverance, then why would they say lessons are learned easier here? Isn't this three-dimensional plane the worst for experiencing physical and emotional pain? The mental and emotional trauma can be excruciatingly paralyzing.

This is definitely for me!!! You wouldn't believe the protection I have tried to embrace myself in. Being a mental and emotional nerve ending doesn't make for a great successful journey through this life. Debilitating is debilitating. Would the world of peace you are talking about be "the Other Side?" Then so be it, no? Answer away!
Mike

First of all, as I've said all along, while I've never heard a soul say that it regretted what it did, at the same time it didn't minimize the act either. The souls talk about regretting, not anything they've done, but what they *didn't* do.

The point that they're trying to make is that they aren't punished by God for what they did, contrary to what is taught by so many religions and denominations.

Secondly, I've never heard a soul recommend it either. You're here on this earth for a reason. The idea that you're feeling like a mental and emotional nerve ending says that you're way off course.

Something else that souls have said to me once, and it was something that literally stopped me in my tracks was, "When someone doesn't like himself, his soul shrivels up." You weren't born to suffer, but to recreate Heaven here on earth, both for others and yourself. God's intention for you is not that you suffer but that you feel fully alive, celebrating the gifts that are yours and the blessings that are around you.

The turmoil you're experiencing is a wakeup call. Every challenge in your life, no matter how great or small is meant for you to look deep inside and bring out the best in you. This is why the souls never say that "self–deliverance" is the way to go either. The souls say that after they do their life review, they see that they did have options available to them that they didn't see at the time, but would have seen had they hung in there a little longer.

We're never given a challenge that is beyond our ability to meet and master, because we're greater than whatever situation we might find ourselves facing. I've heard the souls say that the reason we come here is to create "Heaven" on earth, in any way we can, for ourselves and others. They've also said that the most difficult experiences we face contain our most insightful lessons. While we're here, our purpose is to bring peace and hope to others, while we're in the midst of our own pain. It's the most important mission we'll accomplish while we're here on earth, and it's the one that will bring us the most reward when we return to the Other Side.

They say that you must find a way to make your way through the pain of loss and confusion and still keep your sense of trust and courage together. Every second you do so earns you a reward so profound that the souls have said that they would gladly go through all of the misery again, even more so, just to have a fraction of the peace, beauty, joy, and love that they've found in their new world. But they say that they had to earn it, and the turmoil they stomached was a small price to pay.

So how do you get back on track? According to the souls, you simply go in the direction your heart tells you. Each of us has a path that matches our spirit. When you follow your heart, you'll find yourself feeling alive and fulfilled, and you'll find the courage to follow the road in front of you just a little farther. Fulfilling the plan you set out for yourself before you came here is important not only for yourself, but to those around you, who will advance on their own journey from watching your example.

If your heart is empty, dissatisfied, or unfulfilled, look deeper. You'll find that the faith and hope you thought were gone have never left you. It's hidden underneath the walls of your fears, insecurities, and loss of purpose. I can tell you as a "spiritual teacher" that while belief in a higher power is necessary, belief in yourself is one of the most important lessons you're to learn while you're here. Never give up on finding and following your truth. Do not compromise on what you know to be real. You are here for a reason, and every day that passes, from this moment on, is a step closer to your dream. You just need the will to hang on to your hope.

Then, when you come to the end of your journey here and finish your life review on the Other Side, the Eternal Light of Love and the souls will say to you, "Well done."

26

What's the Point?

This book is based on a seminar I conduct entitled, "Lessons from the Other Side." What I teach in it is grounded on what the souls have shown, and told me, about their life on the Other Side. As part of the workshop I lead the attendees through a guided meditation of the hereafter. I walk them through a dim reflection of what the souls have revealed to me that the Other Side is like.

When the meditation is over, I'm not surprised to see men, along with women, in tears as they're reminded from where they've come. I've been told that the meditation has helped ease the grief and pain of loss people were feeling because they have an idea of what the world their loved ones live in is like, and they feel the joy.

"So why would anyone leave what you've just experienced to come this spiritual cesspool?" I ask when the meditation is done.

"Because we want to," I'll say, answering my own question.

The souls have explained to me that before we come to earth, we take into consideration what lesson we need to learn in order to "advance" in our spiritual growth on the Other Side. We plan a journey that will test not only our ability to love and to forgive but also our faith, our resolve, our spirituality, and our very humanity while we're here. We come here to learn lessons that determine the circumstances of our lives during which some of us will discover how to be humble, others will realize how to live with the outcomes that come from making bad decisions, others will absorb the lessons acquired from positions of power, and still others will assimilate lessons of love and of being loved.

We come here to experience what we aren't capable of on the Other Side. Death doesn't exist in the hereafter, but we come here, knowing we will lose loved ones, to learn the lessons that grief can teach us. No one gets in our face on the Other Side, so we also come here to learn lessons in forgiveness when people do. We leave the loving, supportive communities that we live in there so that we can learn lessons that can only be learned from being betrayed, losing a loved one to death, and so forth.

So we come here knowing that it's going to be a struggle and that we're going to be hurt, but we also know that the time we're here on earth is limited. We hope that the conflict and ache we face and feel will cause us to grow spiritually because we have a predetermined amount of time before we return home again, and that in the end it'll all be worthwhile.

While the lessons we are here to learn are as varied as those who walk the face of this planet, we all share the common purposes of reflecting the Eternal Light of Love to one another and creating Heaven on earth. Whatever are the lessons we came here to learn, we want to learn them because by doing so we're able to understand and experience the peace, joy, and love the Eternal Light of Love has for each and every one of us. And every soul wants to be loved.

What about people who don't know why they're here?

Hi, Anthony,
In the fifty years I've lived, I've never discovered my purpose. I feel as
though I'm roaming around purposelessly. Nothing's ever sparked me like,

"Maybe that's the reason I'm here." In your experience, are there a lot of
people out there like me?
Audrey

Saint Francis of Assisi was gardening one day when he was asked
what he would do if he found out he had only one more hour to live.
He thought about it for a moment and answered, "I'd keep on gardening."

Martin Luther King, Jr. was asked what he would do if he knew he
had only one more day to live, and he said, "I'd plant a tree."

Both of these men changed the world, but they both understood
what their real purpose was—to live life so well that when death comes
you don't even notice it. You just go from this life to an even greater
life in the hereafter.

We all come here to learn lessons, and according to the souls, any
part of our lives that goes unlived is a lesson that hasn't been learned.
Not learning all of the lessons we came here to acquire is what causes
us to feel as though we're wandering around "aimlessly." The souls say
that what's crucial to success in our life and the lessons we're to learn
while we're here is to gain an understanding of who we are, who we
were, and what the potential is within us that has yet to be realized. In
other words, knowing what we want and who we want to be.

It's been said that at the end of our lives we don't regret what we've
done but what we didn't do. The souls are constantly agreeing with
that notion. They talk about their regret at not having done more for
themselves or not being more of who they could have been while
they were here on earth. Yes, they say that when they arrive in the
hereafter, they do find what eluded them while they were alive here,
but at the same time they say it would have been nice to have lived
their lives to the fullest *before* they made the transition from this life.
When they look back on what could have been, they shake their heads
and wonder why they didn't put aside their guilt and fears and grab
with both hands the happiness that was available to them. They often
talk about how easy this would have been to do if they'd only quit
selling themselves and their lives short. I've heard them say that when
they look back on their lives, they have wondered what their worry
was all about. Instead of pedaling faster to keep up, they could have

soared beyond the limitations of fear and uncertainty and guilt which imprisoned them.

Fear is what is behind our decision not to follow our passions in order to pursue the things we love. We do not accomplish what we want to achieve nor do we become the people we want to be. What this all points to is not that we are victims of circumstance as we might want to believe, but that we lack the faith in ourselves to be who we are meant to be. Instead of living our lives from *inspiration*, we find ourselves living from *desperation*.

So what can you do to change course and discover the reason why you're here? First of all, the souls say, embrace all of your experiences and lessons while you're here on earth —the good, the bad, the magnificent, and the disastrous—because everything happens to help you grow spiritually.

Secondly, the souls say that you need to remember that while you love your spouse, children, family, and friends, their journey is *their* journey, and your journey is *your* journey. No one's journey is more important than your own. No one can learn for you the spiritual lessons that you came here to attain, nor can anyone else finish the journey that you came here to experience. While helping someone else feels good and brings you joy, you risk forgetting why you're here by involving yourself in someone else's life to the point of losing your way in your own life. You can still be a mother, daughter, or friend and accomplish the goals you came here to achieve in order to receive the most all-inclusive education while you're here on earth.

Live the life you chose to live while you're here. Follow your passion; it's the voice of the Eternal Light of Love reminding you of why you came here to begin with. When you follow your heart and stay true to your passion while pursuing your own unique path, death will never be able to touch you. Celebrate your heart's desires and you'll recreate Heaven here on earth and reflect the Eternal Light of Love to everyone you touch; and that, according to the souls, is the purpose of life here on earth.

27

I Told You So!

I cannot tell you how many times I've heard, "I wish I could be you for a day." I usually answer, "So do I. I could use the break."

I just had a great conversation with Barb over Facebook messenger. She said she wished she were a medium because even though she received a reading from me . . . *"You did a reading for me and I was astounded because you said some things only my family would know, left me speechless and me being speechless is really hard to do . . . there still was, there still is, that little bit of doubt ~ call me 'doubting Thomas.' Now if one of those spirits would just appear in front of me, I would be sold and then I would faint dead away. LOL!"*

The souls of her loved ones, and yours, would tell you that doubt is natural. The purpose of a medium session isn't to take away your grief or doubt, but to give you the assurance that "death is not the end of life, love, or relationships."

The souls say that if God took away all of our doubts and revealed all of the answers we're asking for, we wouldn't then absorb the lessons we came here to learn.

Some people seem to think that because of my ability I breeze through life. Nothing could be further from the truth. After doing countless numbers of sessions, acting as a "bridge" between this life and the hereafter, I still have questions without answers and struggles that leave me breathless.

Even after all these years of doing this work, while I don't doubt the existence of the Other Side, it doesn't mean I have all of the answers to life here. If anything, because I no longer struggle with the existence of life after death, it's deepened my questions about my life *before* death.

The souls say that one of the things they want us to know is that all of our questions will be answered in the hereafter. They want us to know that they are happy and at peace.

They also want us to know that our life there will directly reflect the lessons we learned, or didn't learn, while we're here. So while we're here, we should be more concerned with learning the lessons we're here to learn. When we've done that, we'll be reunited with our loved ones on the Other Side, and all doubt will disappear.

But I'll be there, wagging my finger at you, saying, "I told you so!"

How can I let my father know I love him?

My stepfather passed December 1st and due to family issues I didn't get to say good-bye or anything. Is there a way I can let him know that I did love him and that I'm sorry for all the stupid stuff?
Shellie

One of the things that the souls stress during the sessions that I do is that they are always with us. They are aware of what is going on in our lives; and like the Eternal Light of Love, they hear everything we say to them, either in thought or in prayer.

It's common for someone to say to me during a session, "Please tell them I love them."

I always say, "You already did." Our loved ones always hear us when we talk to them. They also know when we think about them and what we're thinking.

I noticed you said, " . . . I did love him . . . " During discernments, the souls talk about their love for you, not "I did love you." That's because their physical body has died, not their love for you.

I cannot tell you how many times I've heard souls say, "Keep talking to me. I can hear you. I'm always with you. I'm here to help whenever you need me. You are never alone."

So you can say what you want to say to any of your loved ones on the Other Side out loud, in your thoughts, or by writing what you're thinking or feeling. My favorite suggestion to make is that you light a candle and say a prayer. As long as that candle is burning, your prayer is being said.

I cannot stress, or say this, enough—the souls use mediums to give them a human voice so that they can communicate with you in a way you can hear and hopefully understand. You *do not* need a medium, or to be one, to communicate with your loved ones on the Other Side, and they don't need one to hear you. All you need to do is open your mouth and start speaking to them.

Epilogue

The souls want you to know that death is not the end, but a beginning . . . We live forever. The life we're living here on earth is just a small part of our journey as eternal beings. As much as you want to know that they're happy on the Other Side, they want to know that you're happy here as well. That's why they will always speak to you and *anyone* who is willing to listen with an open heart.

They know what you need in order for you to stay on your path, to keep the spark of hope alive within you, and to help you put one foot in front of the other on your journey through grief.

What the souls also want you to know is that when it's your time to make the journey from this life to the next, there's nothing you need to be afraid of. The moment is one of tremendous peace without any struggle. Whatever pain or suffering you may have gone through on earth will now end immediately. You'll be welcomed to a setting which is so comforting that you can't help but be drawn to it. They describe this home as peaceful and luminous, without pain, sorrow, tears, anger, or regret. They talk of being unconditionally loved and accepted. It's the *home* that you'll find yourself wanting to be a part of.

As I said at the start, there is a reason for everything that happens, and the reason is that we are all on a journey into the heart of the Eternal Light of Love. And as we do so, it becomes clearer to us that the purpose of our lives and our spiritual journey is coming *home*, where we truly belong.

Afterword

I noticed a "trend," at least in my sessions. When I'm discerning a soul, I ask it a number of questions:

- What is your name?
- How are you related to the "sitter?"
- How did you transition?
- What can you tell me about yourself?
- What do you want your loved one to know?

These are just a few of them. This is the "getting to know you" part of the session for me.

What I have noticed was an increasing reluctance on the part of the souls to talk about their passing. I'll never forget the one soul who told me, "What does it matter? I was there; now I'm here."

Since then I've heard things like: "I didn't die. I just changed addresses."

155

"The events that led to my being here came together beautifully."

Feeling it was an important piece of evidence in a session, I became frustrated enough to tell one soul that his mother really needed to hear it so she'll know it was really him. "She knows it's me. Besides, talking about it will only bring up more pain. What difference does it make how I got here? The important thing is that she remembers my life while I was there. That's what I want her to remember. Our life together while I was there."

As a medium I can tell you this: your loved ones on the Other Side know that you're missing them, but they'd want you to give thanks for the time that you had together. They'd want you, as much as you can in your grief, to appreciate their life, your life together, and the lives of all your loved ones still here with you.

They want you to know that they're giving thanks for you being a part of their lives, and that whoever they were to you in this life, they still are now. Death is not the end of life, love, or relationships.

While they're grateful for the time and lessons they learned here on earth, they're also grateful for being back at home where they're waiting for you.

The souls and I would like to suggest that as much as possible, give thanks for your life together and their life now in a place of peace, love, and joy. And from that place, put one foot in front of the other during your journey through grief, knowing that you are *never* alone.

I Never Went Away

I stood by your bed last night
I came to have a peep
I could see that you were crying
You found it hard to sleep

I whined to you softly
As you brushed away a tear
It's "me" I haven't left you
I'm well, I'm fine, I'm here

I was close to you at breakfast
I watched you pour your tea
You were thinking of the many times
Your hands reached down to me

I was with you at the shops today
Your arms were getting sore
I longed to take your parcels
I wish I could do more

I was with you at my grave today
You tend it with such care
I want to reassure you
That I am not lying there

I walked with you towards the house
As you fumbled for the key
I gently put my [hand] on you
I smiled and said "it's me"

You looked so very tired
As you sank into a chair
I tried so hard to let you know
That I was standing there

It's possible for me
To be so near every day
To say to you with certainty
"I never went away"

You sat there very quietly
Then smiled like you knew
In the stillness of the evening
I was very close to you

The day is over
I smile at you yawning
And say goodnight, God bless
I'll see you in the morning

And when the time is right for you
To cross the brief divide
I'll rush across to meet you
And we'll stand side by side

I have so many things to show you
There is so much for you to see
Be patient, live your journey out
Then come home to be with me

Anonymous [Text adapted by the author.]

4TH DIMENSION PRESS

An Imprint of A.R.E. Press

4th Dimension Press is an imprint of A.R.E. Press, the publishing division of Edgar Cayce's Association for Research and Enlightenment (A.R.E.).

We publish books, DVDs, and CDs in the fields of intuition, psychic abilities, ancient mysteries, philosophy, comparative religious studies, personal and spiritual development, and holistic health.

For more information, or to receive a catalog, contact us by mail, phone, or online at:

4th Dimension Press
215 67th Street
Virginia Beach, VA 23451-2061
800-333-4499

4THDIMENSIONPRESS.COM

Who Was Edgar Cayce?
Twentieth Century Psychic and Medical Clairvoyant

Edgar Cayce (pronounced Kay-Cee, 1877-1945) has been called the "sleeping prophet," the "father of holistic medicine," and the most-documented psychic of the 20th century. For more than 40 years of his adult life, Cayce gave psychic "readings" to thousands of seekers while in an unconscious state, diagnosing illnesses and revealing lives lived in the past and prophecies yet to come. But who, exactly, was Edgar Cayce?

Cayce was born on a farm in Hopkinsville, Kentucky, in 1877, and his psychic abilities began to appear as early as his childhood. He was able to see and talk to his late grandfather's spirit, and often played with "imaginary friends" whom he said were spirits on the other side. He also displayed an uncanny ability to memorize the pages of a book simply by sleeping on it. These gifts labeled the young Cayce as strange, but all Cayce really wanted was to help others, especially children.

Later in life, Cayce would find that he had the ability to put himself into a sleep-like state by lying down on a couch, closing his eyes, and folding his hands over his stomach. In this state of relaxation and meditation, he was able to place his mind in contact with all time and space—the universal consciousness, also known as the super-conscious mind. From there, he could respond to questions as broad as, "What are the secrets of the universe?" and "What is my purpose in life?" to as specific as, "What can I do to help my arthritis?" and "How were the pyramids of Egypt built?" His responses to these questions came to be called "readings," and their insights offer practical help and advice to individuals even today.

The majority of Edgar Cayce's readings deal with holistic health and the treatment of illness. Yet, although best known for this material, the sleeping Cayce did not seem to be limited to concerns about the physical body. In fact, in their entirety, the readings discuss an astonishing 10,000 different topics. This vast array of subject matter can be narrowed down into a smaller group of topics that, when compiled together, deal with the following five categories: (1) Health-Related Information; (2) Philosophy and Reincarnation; (3) Dreams and Dream Interpretation; (4) ESP and Psychic Phenomena; and (5) Spiritual Growth, Meditation, and Prayer.

Learn more at EdgarCayce.org.

What Is A.R.E.?

Edgar Cayce founded the non-profit Association for Research and Enlightenment (A.R.E.) in 1931, to explore spirituality, holistic health, intuition, dream interpretation, psychic development, reincarnation, and ancient mysteries—all subjects that frequently came up in the more than 14,000 documented psychic readings given by Cayce.

The Mission of the A.R.E. is to help people transform their lives for the better, through research, education, and application of core concepts found in the Edgar Cayce readings and kindred materials that seek to manifest the love of God and all people and promote the purposefulness of life, the oneness of God, the spiritual nature of humankind, and the connection of body, mind, and spirit.

With an international headquarters in Virginia Beach, Va., a regional headquarters in Houston, regional representatives throughout the U.S., Edgar Cayce Centers in more than thirty countries, and individual members in more than seventy countries, the A.R.E. community is a global network of individuals.

A.R.E. conferences, international tours, camps for children and adults, regional activities, and study groups allow like-minded people to gather for educational and fellowship opportunities worldwide.

A.R.E. offers membership benefits and services that include a quarterly body-mind-spirit member magazine, *Venture Inward*, a member newsletter covering the major topics of the readings, and access to the entire set of readings in an exclusive online database.

Learn more at EdgarCayce.org.

EDGARCAYCE.ORG